LONDON'S
VILLAGE WALKS

20 Walks Around the City's Most Interesting Historic Villages

by David Hampshire

T0159587

City Books • Bath • England

First published 2018

Copyright © Survival Books 2018
Cover design: Survival Books
Cover photo: Hampstead Village
Maps © Jim Watson

City Books, c/o Survival Books Limited
Office 169, 3 Edgar Buildings
George Street, Bath BA1 2FJ, United Kingdom
+44 (0)1305-266918
info@survivalbooks.net
www.survivalbooks.net and www.londons-secrets.com

British Library Cataloguing in Publication Data
A CIP record for this book is available
from the British Library

ISBN: 978-1-909282-94-0

Printed in China

Acknowledgements

The author would like to thank all the many people who helped with research and provided information for this book. Special thanks are due to Alex Browning for her invaluable research, Graeme & Louise Chesters and Richard Todd; Robbi Forrester Atilgan for editing; Peter Read for additional editing and proof-reading; Susan Griffith for final proof checking; John Marshall for DTP, photo selection and cover design; and Jim Watson for the lovely maps.

Last, but not least, a special thank you to the many photographers – the unsung heroes – whose beautiful images bring London to life.

Author's Notes

Please note the following regarding the walks in this book.

♦ **Length & Duration:** The length of walks is approximate – shown to the nearest quarter mile – as is the time required to complete them, particularly if you make a lot of stops (coffee, lunch, museums, shopping, etc.). The average walking speed is around 3mph but we have allowed for a much slower pace of 2mph. (The idea isn't to get from the start to finish as quickly as possible.) You can, of course, start a walk from either end and combine a number of walks to make a longer walk, or alternatively, shorten a walk. Most walks are graded easy or moderate with relatively few steep hills or steps.

♦ **Opening Hours:** Most of the buildings and public spaces (e.g. parks) included in the walks are open seven days a week; opening times may vary for weekdays/weekends and by season. Almost all parks and gardens offer free access, unless otherwise indicated. The opening hours of many sights and museums (etc.) are listed, though these are liable to change. Where there's an entry fee, it's noted.

♦ **Transport:** All walks start and end at or near a tube or railway station. Most can also be reached by bus (routes aren't listed as there are simply too many to include them all) and sometimes by river ferry. The postcode of the starting point is shown should you wish to drive. However, the nearest car park or on-road parking may be some distance away, particularly in central London – and can be expensive.

♦ **Maps:** The maps aren't drawn to scale. Points of interest are numbered. An overall map of London is included on pages 8-9, showing the location of walks within the city.

♦ **Food & Drink:** Recommended 'pit stops' have been included in all walks – shown in yellow in the map key and in the text (other food and drink places are numbered as landmarks but aren't specifically recommended). When not listed, a pub/restaurant's meal times are usually the 'standard' hours, e.g. noon-2.30 or 3pm and 6-11pm, although some are open all day and may also serve food all day (as do cafés). Many pubs are also open in the mornings for coffee, etc. Telephone numbers are listed where bookings are advisable or necessary, otherwise booking isn't usually required or even possible. Note that in the City of London, many establishments are open only from Monday to Friday. A price guide is included (£ = inexpensive, ££ = moderate, £££ = expensive); most recommended places fall into the inexpensive category.

Contents

Camden Passage, Islington

Introduction

The largest city in Western Europe (west of Istanbul), Greater London covers an area of over 600mi² (ca. 1,600km²) and has a population of almost 9 million. Unlike more modern cities, London wasn't planned logically but grew organically. From its beginnings as a Roman trading port some 2,000 years ago, it has mushroomed into the metropolis we see today, swallowing up thousands of villages, hamlets and settlements in the process. Many former villages – like Bloomsbury and Notting Hill – are now bustling cosmopolitan neighbourhoods, while others, such as Barnes and Dulwich, retain much of their original rural charm and character.

You might dispute some areas' village status nowadays, but back in the 18th and 19th centuries, people were farming in Islington, fishing in Chiswick and building country piles in Hoxton. Patronage from royalty and wealthy merchants helped to boost the profile of some villages, while new migrants set up home-from-home 'villages' in areas such as Spitalfields. The city began to grow in earnest in the late 18th and early 19th centuries and the pace increased ten-fold with the advent of the railways in the 1840s, which saw dozens of villages devoured by the advancing city. Between 1801 and 1891, London's population increased from barely a million to over 5½ million.

Nevertheless, if you're seeking a village vibe – a green on which to watch cricket, lots of small independent shops, a market selling local farmers' produce, an ancient church and graveyard to explore, a pub with a warm welcome (and local ales and ducks paddling in the pond outside) – you can still find them if you know where to look. Scratch beneath the surface of modern London and you'll find a rich tapestry of ancient villages, just waiting to be rediscovered.

London's Village Walks explores 20 of the city's most interesting and best preserved 'villages', where – with a little imagination – it's still possible to picture yourself living in a bygone age. The walks are between 2 and 6½ miles in length, with the average around 4 miles. However, it's best to allow half a day for the shorter walks and as much as a full day for the longer walks – particularly if you plan to partake of the many excellent pubs, restaurants and cafés along the routes (for your author, a good lunch is a prerequisite of a good walk!) – not to mention the many diversions along the way, such as museums, galleries and churches. The aim is to take the 'scenic route', visiting as many interesting landmarks as possible, rather than simply getting from A to B as fast as possible.

Writing *London's Village Walks* has been a fascinating, educational and enjoyable journey of discovery. We hope that you enjoy these walks as much as we did; all you need is a comfortable pair of shoes, a sense of adventure – and this book!

David Hampshire
April 2018

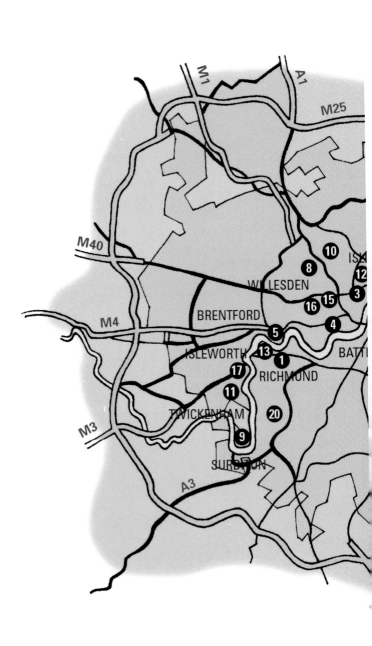

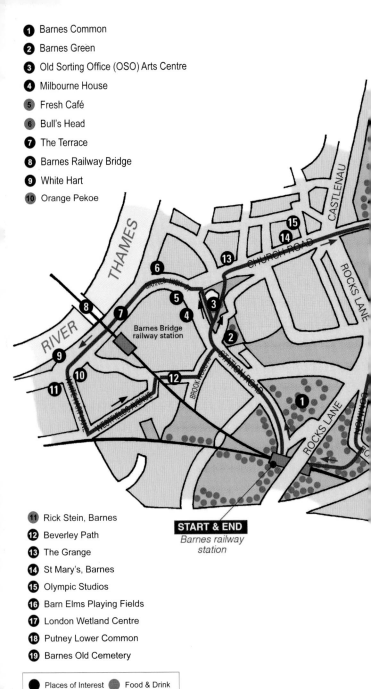

1. Barnes Common
2. Barnes Green
3. Old Sorting Office (OSO) Arts Centre
4. Milbourne House
5. Fresh Café
6. Bull's Head
7. The Terrace
8. Barnes Railway Bridge
9. White Hart
10. Orange Pekoe
11. Rick Stein, Barnes
12. Beverley Path
13. The Grange
14. St Mary's, Barnes
15. Olympic Studios
16. Barn Elms Playing Fields
17. London Wetland Centre
18. Putney Lower Common
19. Barnes Old Cemetery

START & END
Barnes railway station

THAMES
RIVER
CASTLENAU
CHURCH ROAD
ROCKS LANE
BARNES HIGH ST
STATION ROAD
BROOK ROAD
WHITE HART LANE
WEST MELBOURNE AVENUE
Barnes Bridge railway station

Places of Interest
Food & Drink

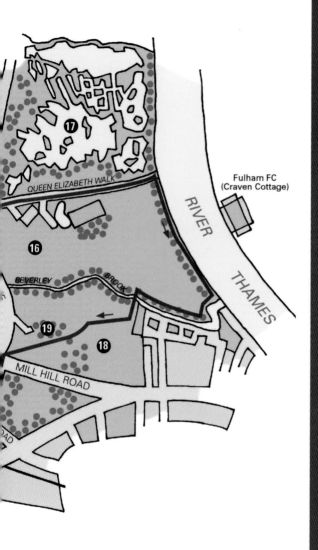

Barnes

Distance: 4½ miles (7 km)
Terrain: easy, some moderate hills
Duration: 2½ hours
Start & End: Barnes rail
Postcode: SW13 0HT

BARNES

Elegant, affluent Barnes sits on the south bank of the River Thames – tucked into an upward loop of the river – with Chiswick to the west, Hammersmith to the north, Putney to the east and Mortlake/Roehampton to the south. One of the most well-heeled and desirable suburbs of southwest London, Barnes has the atmosphere of a quintessential country village and is noted for its strong sense of community, expansive green spaces and beautiful riverside walks.

This ancient rural enclave appears in the *Domesday Book* of 1086 as Berne (barn). Until the mid-19th century the village comprised just a few shops and inns, with some imposing houses around the green and common, but it grew rapidly after the construction of Hammersmith Bridge (1827) and the railway (1846). Although less than 6 miles (ca. 10km) from central London and located within the London borough of Richmond-upon-Thames, Barnes still feels like a country village – complete with village green and duck pond – much of which is protected as a conservation area. It has many handsome riverside pubs, fine restaurants and cosy cafés and a wealth of traditional independent stores (Barnes reportedly has the highest proportion of indie traders of any town in Britain).

Barnes is also noted for its abundance of beautiful architecture, predominantly from the 18th and 19th centuries, with areas characterised by certain styles. Of particular interest is The Terrace, which is lined with splendid early 18th-century waterfront properties overlooking the Thames; look out for its majestic 'lion houses' (dating from the late 1890s), with their fine detailing and proud lions peering down from their rooftop perches. 'Little Chelsea' offers quaint bijou Victorian terraced houses, in contrast to the sleek luxurious apartments and townhouses that are emerging around the village.

Our walk traverses Barnes Common and Green, makes a tour of the village (and its most popular streets), explores sections of the Thames Path, and takes us around and across Putney Common and along the lovely Beverley Brook, before terminating back at Barnes railway station.

Start Walking…

Leaving Barnes station, go left on Station Road across glorious **Barnes Common ❶** , passing the cricket ground on your left. The Common covers around 124 acres (50ha) – one of the largest areas of unenclosed common land within easy reach of central London – and was mainly marshland until drained in the late 19th century. It's now a Local Nature Reserve, comprising open grassland, trees and woodland, home to an abundance of flora and fauna; it's noted for its grasses but has few mammals due to its open nature.

After around 300m you pass some houses on the left (after

> ### Barnes Green
>
> At the heart of the community, the Green is a delightful tranquil spot with a large pond; it's the venue for several open-air events (including Barnes Fair in July and the Barnes Food Fair in September) and regular covered markets. In former times the stocks were located here and during medieval fairs there were races around the pond. Today it's a popular venue for ball games, picnics and feeding the ducks, and is home to the Barnes Green Social Centre, the Old Sorting Office Arts Centre and Barnes Methodist Church (1906).

Scarf Road) and soon after you cross over Beverley Brook just before **Barnes Green ❷** (see box above). Beverley Brook is an 8-mile (13km) river rising in Worcester Park and entering the Thames near Leader's Gardens on the Putney Embankment. (The Beverley Brook Walk follows much of the river's course – see www.merton.gov.uk/assets/Documents/beverly-brook-walk.pdf).

Continue along the left edge of the Green and follow the path past the **Old Sorting Office (OSO) Arts Centre ❸** and the Wildwood restaurant (both good places for coffee or lunch). Opposite the

Barnes Green

The Terrace

Arts Centre, on the other side of Station Road, is 17th-century **Milbourne House** ❹, former home of the author Henry Fielding (1707-54), creator of Tom Jones. Marked by a blue plaque, it's the oldest private residence in Barnes and incorporates parts of an earlier Tudor building, including an Elizabethan fireplace in the entrance hall. Next door is Essex House, now a doctors' surgery and the venue for Barnes weekly Farmers' Market which takes place in the car park (Sat, 10am-2pm). Just around the corner on Church Road, opposite the duck pond, is the 18th-century Sun Inn, a large rambling establishment occupying a striking whitewashed building with an expansive terrace. At the rear of the inn is Barnes Bowling Club, where Sir Francis Drake is said to have taught Elizabeth I to play bowls.

Turn left from Station Road along Barnes High Street where, on the right, the Barnes Community Organisation occupies 17th-century Rose House, formerly a tiny pub. The **Fresh Café** ❺ at number 4 is a good place to get a caffeine fix. At the end of the street you arrive at the riverside – the **Bull's Head** ❻ pub on the right, facing the Thames, has been one of the UK's premier jazz venues for the last 60 years – and head left along **The Terrace** ❼. This handsome street is lined with elegant pastel-coloured Georgian houses overlooking a wide and peaceful stretch of the Thames. The houses date from 1720 and encompass a variety of architectural styles, many replete with porticos and verandas. Number 10 on the corner of Cleveland Gardens has a blue plaque to the composer Gustav Holst (1874-1934) who lived here from 1907-13 when he was head of music at St Paul's Girls' School. The house has a large music room on the top floor and a terrace where Holst and fellow composer Ralph Vaughan Williams would watch the University Boat Race.

Thames Path

The Thames Path (www.nationaltrail.co.uk/thames-path) is a long-distance National Trail footpath running for 184 miles (296km) along the banks of the River Thames. From its source in the Cotswold hills to the Thames Flood Barrier at Woolwich in southeast London, it flows through peaceful water meadows, unspoilt rural villages, historic towns and cities, and finally through the heart of London.

Continue along the Thames Path (see box, left) under **Barnes Railway Bridge** ❽ (1895, Grade II listed) – the original bridge built in 1849 still stands on the upstream side – opposite Barnes Bridge railway station. At the end of The Terrace is the **White Hart** ❾, a historic Young's pub dating from the 1660s with a large bar, roaring fire and wonderful river views; it's a prime spot from which to watch the climax of the Boat Race as the crews from Oxford and Cambridge Universities push for the finish every spring, as they have done for almost 200 years (see www.theboatrace.org). Turn left past the White Hart into White Hart Lane passing **Orange Pekoe** ❿ on your left (a temple to tea established in 2006), while opposite is **Rick Stein, Barnes** ⓫, an outpost of the eponymous TV chef's empire.

Continue along White Hart Lane – the area here is known as Little Chelsea – a popular street lined with shops and pretty terraced cottages, which marks the the boundary between Barnes and Mortlake. Among the many

businesses here are Annie's Barnes, a Bohemian restaurant at number 36, and Tobias & the Angel, a delightful home furnishings shop, at number 66. Opposite the China Chef restaurant, turn left into Westfields Avenue where you pass some allotments, the remnants of the former market gardens of Westfields. Just before the end of the street take the Long Walk footpath on the left and after 50m turn right along **Beverley Path** ⓬, an ancient route between Mortlake and Putney which crosses land known as the Goslings (recorded in 1464 as Geseland, where geese were reared). After around 150m go left into Brookwood Avenue, walk to the end and cross over Station Road and back to Barnes Green.

Follow the path along the right-hand side of the Green and turn right to pass between the pond (on your left) and the Barnes Green Social Centre. As you exit onto Church Road, turn right and some 50m along on the left, just past Nassau Road, is **The Grange** ⓭, an 18th-century house with attractive early 19th-century railings. Next door is St Osmund's Catholic Primary School, established around 1900 by French nuns.

Turn right along Church Road to browse one of Barnes' main shopping streets. Outlets here include Gail's Bakery, Ginger Pig (an excellent butcher) and a delightfully named greengrocer, Two Peas in a Pod. Just past Kitson Road is **St Mary's, Barnes** ⓮, a handsome medieval church

Beverley Brook

Walk 1

St Mary's, Barnes

with a fascinating history, lovely churchyard and a coffee shop. The church's oldest parts include the 12th-century Langton Chapel (named after Archbishop Stephen Langton, who dedicated the church in 1215) and the brick-built west tower constructed around 1485. Next door to the church is another fine Georgian building, Strawberry House, followed by **Olympic Studios** ⓯ , one of London's best boutique art-house cinemas, complete with a café and restaurant. The building has had a chequered history as a village hall, concert hall, cinema, theatre and – most famously – a recording studio from 1966 to 2009. In its heyday it played host to many of rock and pop's greatest stars, including the Rolling Stones, Jimi Hendrix, the Beatles, David Bowie, Queen, Pink Floyd and Madonna.

Continue along Church Road to the busy junction with Rocks Lane and Castelnau – which means 'new castle' in the Occitan language – and cross over to Queen Elizabeth Walk. On the right are **Barn Elms Playing Fields** ⓰ , on land that once

belonged to the Archbishop of Canterbury. A manor house on the site (Barn Elms) was once owned by Sir Francis Walsingham – Elizabeth I's spymaster – and later the Hoare banking family, who sold it in 1827; it was demolished in 1954, although one of the entrance lodges still survives. The reserve is now part of Putney Common, which stretches from the **London Wetland Centre** ⓱ (see box, below) in the north to Barnes Common; it's a haven for rare flora and fauna (and people!) and has been a popular retreat for centuries.

London Wetland Centre

The WWT London Wetland Centre (entrance fee) covers an area of over 100 acres (40ha), an unexpectedly large wildlife habitat close to central London, and Europe's best urban wildlife-viewing area. The Centre was created by the Wildfowl and Wetlands Trust (WWT) when four concrete reservoirs become redundant after the completion of the Thames Water Ring Main in the '90s. It took five years to establish the centre – during which 300,000 plants and 27,000 trees were planted – which opened in May 2000. (For more information, see www.wwt.org.uk/wetland-centres/london.)

From the Wetland Centre walk along the path that runs parallel to Queen Elizabeth Walk to the river, where you turn right to re-join the Thames Path. On the opposite bank in Putney is Craven Cottage, home to Fulham Football Club, and Bishop's Park and Palace. After around 500m a small bridge crosses Beverley Brook. Take the path to the right just before the

Food & Drink

On the southern edge of the common, close to where Gipsy Road meets Queen's Ride, is a memorial to the rock star Mark Bolan, who was killed in a car crash here in 1977.

⑤ Fresh Café: At number 4 Barnes High Street, Fresh is a good place to get your morning caffeine fix (8am-5pm. £).

⑥ Bull's Head: Popular spot for a traditional pub lunch, particularly on a Sunday when there's live jazz (11am or noon-11/11.30pm, £).

⑩ Orange Pekoe: Cosy venue for afternoon tea – or coffee (7.30am-5pm, 9am weekends, £).

⑪ Rick Stein, Barnes: Lovely restaurant occupying former council stables, RSB offers superb fresh seafood (020-8878 9462, noon-3pm/6-10pm, ££).

and a number of distinguished Victorians are interred here, where an abundance of monuments and statues were erected to their memory. Today it's one of London's forgotten cemeteries, overgrown with trees and shrubs, with many monuments vandalised and statues decapitated. It's a sorry sight, but also hauntingly beautiful, atmospheric and evocative, with an air of gentle decay and quiet seclusion. (There's another historic cemetery – Putney Lower Common Cemetery – in the southeast corner of the common.)

Walk southwest from the cemetery to reach the crossroads of Mill Hill Road and Rocks Lane, then continue along Rocks Lane to Station Road and follow it back to Barnes railway station and the end of the walk.

bridge, which follows the course of the brook for around 400m, after which you cross over a modern bridge on the left to **Putney Lower Common** ⑱. Take the second path on the right, which leads past **Barnes Old Cemetery** ⑲ and Rocks Lane Barnes sports centre.

The cemetery was established in 1854 on 2 acres (0.8ha)

London Wetland Centre

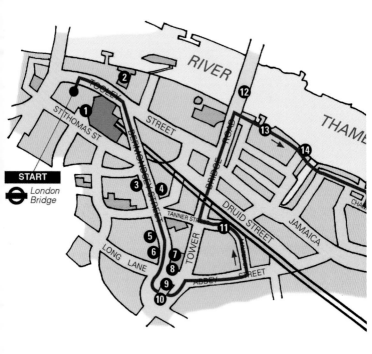

1	Shard	**11**	Maltby Street Market
2	Hay's Galleria	**12**	Tower Bridge
3	London Glassblowing Studio & Gallery	**13**	Shad Thames
4	Fashion & Textile Museum	**14**	Blueprint Café
5	White Cube	**15**	Edward III's Manor House
6	Pizarro	**16**	King's Stairs Gardens
7	St Mary Magdalen	**17**	St Mary's Rotherhithe
8	Watch House	**18**	Mayflower
9	Bermondsey Square	**19**	Brunel Museum
10	Bermondsey Antiques Market		

● Places of Interest   ● Food & Drink

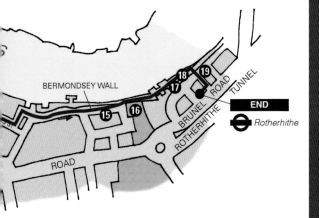

BERMONDSEY WALL

15

16

17

18

19

BRUNEL ROAD

ROTHERHITHE TUNNEL

ROAD

END

Rotherhithe

WALK 2

Bermondsey & Rotherhithe

Distance: 3 miles (5 km)
Terrain: easy, mostly flat terrain
Duration: 1½ hours
Start: London Bridge tube
End: Rotherhithe rail
Postcode: SE1 3QX

Bermondsey is one of the oldest parts of Southwark – and London – with evidence of occupation going back to Roman times. It appears in the *Domesday Book* of 1086 as Bermundesy and Bermundesye, and is thought to be named after Beormund, the Saxon lord of the district. Its Thameside location made it an important transport hub for trade – the borough had the reputation for being the 'Larder of London' – and its riverbank was lined with wharves and warehouses. For many years Bermondsey was famous for its tanneries; by the end of the 18th century a third of all the country's leather came from the area, and this left a legacy of fine industrial buildings.

Once one of London's most insalubrious slums (it was the backdrop for Dickens's *Oliver Twist*), Bermondsey has gone from bust to boom in a generation, its derelict warehouses converted in the '80s into stylish lofts and commercial spaces, restaurants, bars, galleries and artists' studios. The Bermondsey village area, centred on Bermondsey Street and Bermondsey Square, has also seen an upsurge in artistic and commercial activity in recent years. Uber trendy, oozing history and derelict chic – but still rough around the edges – it's now one of the city's most exciting and atmospheric areas and a honeypot for foodies and culture seekers.

The word Rotherhithe is Anglo Saxon in origin and means 'landing place for cattle'. It was originally a low-lying area known as Redriff, with a tight-knit community of shipbuilders and sailors (until the docks closed in 1970). Rotherhithe Street is a rare complete 18th-century village, full of atmosphere and history, now a conservation area. To some, the contrast between original and more gentrified areas is jarring, but it gives the area a unique charm.

Highlights of the walk

Highlights of the walk include the Shard, Hay's Galleria, Bermondsey Street and Square, Maltby Street Market, Tower Bridge, Shad Thames, Rotherhithe Street and the Brunel Museum, along with a wealth of historic buildings and churches, beautiful parks and gardens, and numerous outstanding cafés, bars, restaurants and pubs.

Start Walking…

The walk commences at London Bridge station, before going on to explore the 'villages' of Bermondsey and Rotherhithe. The station has its own claim to fame for train spotters, as the starting point for the London and Greenwich Railway, which opened in 1836 and was the first steam railway in the capital and the first built specifically to carry passengers.

Leave London Bridge tube and exit via London Bridge Walk onto Tooley Street and turn right. If you look to your right you'll see (you can hardly miss it!) London's newest skyscraper, the **Shard ❶** , completed in 2012 and, at 1,016ft (309.6m), the tallest building not only in the UK but in Western Europe. Designed by Italian architect and engineer Renzo Piano, it's a building with multiple uses; a vertical city comprising offices, award-winning restaurants, the 5-star Shangri-La Hotel, exclusive residences, and the UK's highest viewing gallery on the 72nd floor (802ft/245m).

Hay's Galleria

A riverside leisure and shopping complex on the south bank of the Thames, Hay's Galleria opened in 1987 as part of the 'London Bridge City' development. Grade II listed, it's a striking blend of historic and modern architecture and is named after its original owner, the merchant Alexander Hay, who acquired the property – then a brewhouse – in 1651. In around 1840, John Humphrey Jr obtained a lease on the property and commissioned William Cubitt to convert it into a 'wharf'. The centrepiece of the Galleria is an acclaimed 60ft (18.3m) kinetic bronze sculpture of a ship, The Navigators, by David Kemp; weighing in at 14 tonnes, it's a bizarre and captivating symphony of moving parts, water jets and fountains.

Opposite the station (near London Bridge) in Tooley Street is the London Bridge Experience. It's an entertaining if macabre 'immersive theatrical experience' bringing together 'history and horror, education and fun' and is based on the often gruesome history of London's oldest river crossings. Turn right along Tooley Street and after some 200m take a left onto Battle

The Shard

Bridge Lane. This is home to **Hay's Galleria** ➋ (see box, page 21) a good place to grab a coffee before embarking on your walk.

On leaving the Galleria, return to Tooley Street, cross over and take the first right along Bermondsey Street and under the long railway bridge. You emerge into a conservation area lined with attractive converted warehouses and a profusion of trendy places to eat and drink, including – in quick succession – Black Swan Yard Coffee at number 37, the excellent Hide at numbers 39-45 – a warehouse cocktail bar – and Tanner & Co restaurant and bar at number 50. At number 62-66 on the right is the **London Glassblowing Studio & Gallery** ➌ , established by Peter Layton in

---

St Mary Magdalen

The first record of the church of St Mary Magdalen is from around 1290, when Mary Magdalen Chapel was in the hands of the Prior and Convent of Bermondsey. The church once formed part of Bermondsey Abbey (formerly the Priory of St Saviour), which at its height rivalled Westminster Abbey and was an economic and spiritual powerhouse, founded in the 8th century. The oldest part of the present building is the tower, parts of which hark back to the late 13th century, although most of the building dates from around 1680.

1976 in Rotherhithe and relocated here in 2009. It was one of the first hot-glass studios in Europe, where visitors can experience – and even learn – the magic of this ancient craft. Note the lovely shop fronts at 68 and 78, the latter dating from the late 17th century.

On the left at number 83 is the colourful **Fashion & Textile Museum** ➍ . Founded by Zandra Rhodes and owned by Newham College, it's housed in a striking building designed by Mexican architect Ricardo Legorreta, with an eye-catching orange and pink exterior. The museum doesn't have a permanent display but showcases a programme of changing exhibitions exploring the worlds of fashion, textiles and jewellery (see www.ftmlondon.org). Around 100m past the museum, you come to Tanner Street Park on the left, a pleasant little park with four tennis courts (free to use). In the southeast corner is a derelict fountain created from the top of the tower of the former St Olave's church in nearby Tooley Street.

Continuing along Bermondsey Street, not far past the park at number 144-152 (on the right) is the **White Cube** ➎ gallery: housed in a vast white (of course!) building, it's the largest commercial gallery in Europe and one of the coolest destinations in the capital. Along the next section there's another feast of eateries, including Village East (modern European, number 171) Via Bermondsey (Italian, number 177) and **Pizarro** ➏ , a superb Spanish restaurant at number

Bermondsey & Rotherhithe

194. Opposite the latter is **St Mary Magdalen ⑦** (see box, left), a lovely historic church, parts of which date from the 13th century. There's also a beautiful former churchyard, which has been a public park since 1870, and an early 19th-century rectory.

On the left-hand corner at the junction with Abbey Street is

Bermondsey Antiques Market

Food & Drink

⑥ Pizarro: Classy Spanish restaurant on Bermondsey Street (020-7378 9455, noon-10.45pm, £-££).

⑧ Watch House: A cosy café (great coffee) housed in a former 19th-century watch house (7am-6pm, 8am weekends, £).

⑭ Blueprint Café: Much more than a café, the Blueprint in Shad Thames is a superb restaurant providing panoramic views over the river (020-7378 7031, generally noon-2.45pm, 6-10pm, but see website for exact hours, £-££).

⑱ Mayflower: An atmospheric pub on Rotherhithe Street with a small restaurant (11am-11pm, £).

the **Watch House ⑧** , a bijou café housed in a striking 19th-century building designed for the guards who protected the graves of St Mary Magdalen churchyard from body-snatchers. It's been beautifully renovated; its original rustic stone walls are enhanced by colourful art and a black-and-white tiled floor. Opposite the church garden is **Bermondsey Square ⑨** , once the site of Bermondsey Abbey, dissolved in 1537 by Henry VIII. If you walk through the square and across Tower Bridge Road, you come to Grange Walk where there are some splendid historic houses: numbers 5 to 11 are late 17th-century, while number 7 incorporates the remains of the east gatehouse of the abbey.

Return to Bermondsey Square – the original Georgian square was redeveloped in the 2000s and only a few old houses remain – which today is best known as the site of **Bermondsey Antiques Market ⑩** (Fridays, 6am-2pm). Part car boot sale and part chic Parisian flea market, it's a good hunting ground for bric-a-brac, collectables, antiques and all manner of bizarre ephemera. Until the '90s, the

Tower Bridge

Constructed between 1886 and 1894, the bridge takes its name from the nearby Tower of London and is a combined bascule − a moveable bridge which 'opens' to allow ships to pass through − and suspension bridge. It's an iconic symbol of London and one of the world's best-known bridges. The bridge houses an exhibition (entrance fee) that uses film, photos and interactive displays to explain why and how the bridge was built; visitors can also see the original lifting machinery in the Victorian engine rooms. The high-level walkways offer stunning views of the Thames and London's landmarks, and incorporate a glass floor offering a unique (if unnerving) spectacle of the bridge.

sunset to sunrise didn't require provenance, was repealed only in 1995. A farmers' market is held here on Saturdays (10am-2pm).

From the Square head east along Abbey Street and after around 250m turn left down Maltby Street, where the area between Millstream Road to the northern end of Ropewalk hosts **Maltby Street Market ⓫** (Sat 9am-4pm, Sun 11am-4pm). It's a lively informal weekend street market, with a combination of railway arch shops, stalls, pop-up bars and eateries. From Maltby Street follow the road around into Tanner Street to Tower Bridge Road, where you turn right, past St John's Church Park and the London City Mission on the left. Cross Tooley Street and head towards **Tower Bridge ⓬** (see box, left), one of the city's most famous landmarks.

Just before you reach the bridge, take the stairway on the right that leads down to the river level. Turn left under the road arch to the riverfront, from where there are magnificent views of nearby City Hall, Minster Court and the Gherkin. Head back under the arch and walk east along **Shad Thames ⓭**, an attractive cobbled walkway fronting one of London's best-preserved stretches of 19th-century warehouses and wharfs, now converted into apartments, restaurants and bars. These were once packed with coffee

market was notorious as a venue where thieves could legally sell their swag with impunity; a royal licence (*marché ouvert*), which meant that goods sold there from

Shad Thames

and tea, grains and spices, their upper floors linked by a lattice of striking, wrought-iron bridges. The architectural critic Nikolaus Pevsner called Shad Thames 'the most dramatic industrial street surviving in London' and it has provided the backdrop for a number of films, from *Oliver!* to *The Elephant Man*.

a '30s Modernist building. Until 2016 it was also the home of the Design Museum (now relocated to Kensington).

Rotherhithe Riverside

Swing left towards the river along Maggie Blake's Cause (next to a florist), which was named after a local community activist who fought against restricting public access to the riverside. Turn right at the end along the invariably windy Butlers Wharf Pier. The wharf, named after an 18th-century grain trader, contains the largest collection of warehouses on the Thames; built in 1871-3, many were converted into apartments and studios in the '70s (the artist David Hockney had a studio here). Around 200m further on you come to the excellent **Blueprint Café** 14 at number 28, housed on the top floor of a former '40s banana warehouse, converted to resemble

Just past the café and Browns Butlers Wharf, the riverside trail leads over a walkway bridging an inlet and continues along Bermondsey Wall West. At the end you must leave the riverside (to circumvent the Tideway East site, part of London's 'super sewer' project), turning right into East Lane, left along Chambers Street and left again after around 200m into Loftie Street. Follow the road round into Bermondsey Wall East, which runs parallel to Bermondsey Beach, passing Cherry Garden Pier. It's difficult to imagine nowadays, but this was a 17th-century 'resort' (visited by Samuel Pepys). The pier was also the spot from where in 1838 J.M.W. Turner painted one of his most famous works, *The Fighting Temeraire*, depicting the final journey of one of the great ships from the Battle

Blueprint Café

of Trafalgar being towed to a ship-breaker's in Rotherhithe.

Just past the pier is a lush patch of green, home to the remains of **Edward III's Manor House** 15. Built 1349-1353 for Edward III (1312-77), who was crowned king in 1327 aged just 14, the manor had two courtyards surrounded by a moat. In front of the green are Diane Gorvin's statues of Dr Alfred Salter (and his family), who dedicated his life to tackling poverty in 19th-century Bermondsey. Opposite the end of Cathay Street is the Angel, a Victorian inn from around 1830, although the original pub that stood here dated back to the 15th century. A little further on you come to **King's Stairs Gardens** 16 (11.5 acres/4.5ha), which opened in 1962 and is one of the last remaining riverside parks in London; it gets its name from Edward III, who used the stairs to access his manor house. The gardens contain mature

St Mary's Rotherhithe

trees, lawns and steep, undulating hillocks, and offer fine views over the river; there's also a popular children's play area (few homes in the area have gardens).

Continuing past the gardens, follow the path around to Elephant Lane – the centre of the old village of Rotherhithe – and take the footpath next to Prince's Tower (an apartment block) which runs parallel with the river to **St Mary's Rotherhithe** 17. An attractive church in yellow/white and red brick sitting among ancient trees, St Mary's has deep roots in England's maritime history, with links to the *Mayflower* and the Pilgrim Fathers. There's been a church here for at least 1,000 years, although the present building was designed by John James (an associate of Sir Christopher Wren) and built by local shipbuilders in 1716. Its nautical connections are reflected in its construction; the barrel roof was made to look like an upturned ship and the supporting pillars are complete tree trunks encased in plaster. The tranquil churchyard is the resting place of the master of the *Mayflower*, Captain Christopher Jones.

Opposite the south gate of the churchyard is a beautiful three-storey house built in the 1690s. St Mary's Rotherhithe Free School (founded in 1613) moved here from its site adjacent to the church in 1797, and the

The Mayflower

Bermondsey & Rotherhithe

building has two statues on first-floor brackets of 18th-century schoolchildren in uniform. Next door is a watch house dating from 1821, where men stood guard over the churchyard to deter body-snatchers ('resurrection men'). Like the watch house for St Mary Magdalen in Bermondsey it, too, houses a tiny café.

Just past the church, fronting the river, is the atmospheric **Mayflower** 18 pub on Rotherhithe Street, named after the Founding Fathers' ship that set sail for the New World from the pub's wharf in 1620. There's been a tavern here since 1550, making it one of the oldest hostelries on the Thames. Back then the pub was called the Shippe; it was known as the Spread Eagle in the 18th century and has only been called the Mayflower since 1957. It's a charming little pub with a black and white frontage and leaded windows, oak beams, wood panelling – and panoramic Thames' views from its rear deck, which juts out over the river.

Just past the Mayflower turn right into Railway Avenue, where on the corner is the **Brunel Museum** 19 (see box, left), one of London's best small museums with an outstanding café. From the museum continue along the Railway Avenue to the end and turn right, where Rotherhithe railway station – and the end of the walk – is just a few steps along.

Brunel Museum

This intriguing museum (entrance fee, 10am-5pm) pays homage to three generations of the legendary Brunel engineering family: Sir Marc Isambard Brunel (1769-1849), his son Isambard Kingdom Brunel (1806-1859) – widely considered to be Britain's greatest ever engineer – and Isambard's second son, Henry Marc Brunel (1842-1903), also a civil engineer. It sits above the Thames Tunnel – built 1825-1843 as the first passenger tunnel under a navigable river – and includes the Brunel Engine House, where steam engines pumped water from the tunnel, and the stunning Grand Entrance Hall, described by Victorians as the Eighth Wonder of the World. A permanent exhibition tells the story of the tunnel, including display panels, models, original artefacts and a video presentation. The museum also has an excellent café and a 'secret' cocktail bar on Fri-Sat, May to September. (For more information visit www.brunel-museum.org.uk.)

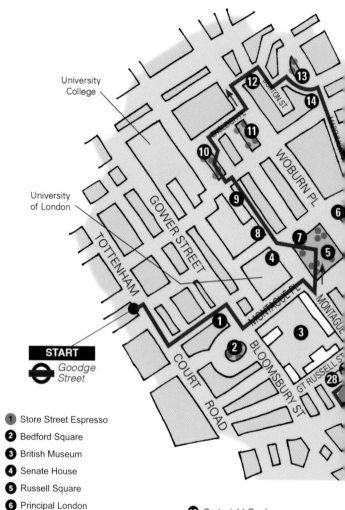

University College

University of London

1 Store Street Espresso
2 Bedford Square
3 British Museum
4 Senate House
5 Russell Square
6 Principal London
7 Cabmen's Shelter
8 Brunel Gallery
9 Woburn Square
10 Gordon Square
11 Tavistock Square
12 Woburn Walk

13 Cartwright Gardens
14 Fork Deli Patisserie
15 Brunswick Centre
16 Brunswick Square Gardens
17 St George's Gardens
18 Foundling Museum
19 Coram's Fields
20 Lamb's Conduit Street

START
Goodge Street

● Places of Interest   ● Food & Drink

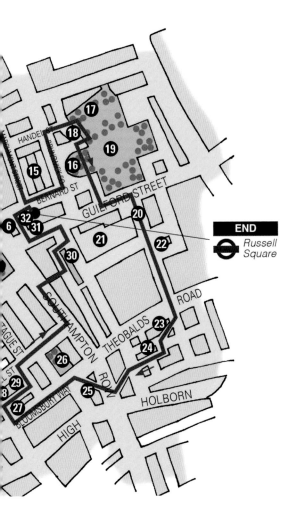

END

Russell Square

21 Great Ormond Street Hospital
22 Lamb
23 Conway Hall
24 Red Lion Square Gardens
25 Sicilian Avenue
26 Bloomsbury Square Garden
27 St George's Bloomsbury
28 Cartoon Museum
29 London Review Bookshop
30 Queen Square
31 Horse Hospital
32 Friend at Hand

Bloomsbury

Distance: 3½ miles (5½ km)
Terrain: easy, flat terrain
Duration: 2 hours
Start: Goodge Street tube
End: Bloomsbury Square tube
Postcode: W1P 9PA

BLOOMSBURY

The intellectual and literary capital of London, beautiful Bloomsbury has some of the city's most extraordinary buildings as well as a bounty of glorious garden squares, most offering free access from dawn to dusk. This area is home to numerous cultural, educational and healthcare institutions, from University College London to the British Museum and Great Ormond Street Hospital. And there's an annual festival in October to celebrate the creativity which blooms in Bloomsbury (http://bloomsburyfestival.org. uk).

Its best-known literary connections include the Bloomsbury Group: a set of artists, intellectuals, philosophers and writers – which included E. M. Forster, John Maynard Keynes, Lytton Strachey and Virginia Woolf – who lived, worked and socialised in Bloomsbury during the first half of the 20th century. It sometimes seems like every other house has a blue plaque to a distinguished writer, scientist or philosopher!

The area's history was first recorded in 1201, when it was acquired by William de Blemond; the name Bloomsbury evolved from Blemondisberi, the 'bury' or manor of Blemond. But it wasn't until the 17th and 18th centuries that Bloomsbury became a fashionable residential district under the stewardship of the Russell family (Dukes of Bedford), whose influence can be seen everywhere today.

Bloomsbury has no official boundaries but can be roughly defined as the 'square' bounded by Tottenham Court Road to the west, Euston Road to the north, Gray's Inn Road to the east, and High Holborn to the south. It's bisected from north to south by the main Southampton Row-Woburn Place thoroughfare, which links Tavistock and Russell Squares – the central points of Bloomsbury.

Bloomsbury

This walk explores some of the city's oldest and loveliest formal squares – dating from the reigns of Charles II through to Victoria – along with a wealth of charming streets, taking in unique shops, fascinating museums, historic pubs, superb cafés and restaurants, and some striking architecture.

Start Walking…

Exit Goodge Street tube station and turn right down Tottenham Court Road and take the second left into Store Street, one of Bloomsbury's most popular shopping streets. If you need a caffeine kick, **Store Street Espresso** ❶ – a handsome, minimalist coffee shop – a few hundred metres up on the right at number 40 is the perfect place. Turn right at the junction with Gower Street and walk south to **Bedford Square** ❷ , the finest surviving Georgian square in London. Most of the houses have been converted into offices – one, on the southeast side, is occupied by the publisher of the

Harry Potter books, Bloomsbury Publishing. The central tree-lined garden remains private.

> ### British Museum
>
> The British Museum (the entrance is in Great Russell Street) is the UK's most popular museum – attracting over 6 million visitors annually – and the fifth most-visited museum in the world. It provides an almost overwhelming smorgasbord of human history and culture stretching across centuries and continents, one that's best appreciated in small bites. The British Museum grew from the private collection of curiosities bequeathed to George II by physician and scientist, Sir Hans Sloane (1660-1753); established in 1753, it was the first national public museum in the world. It's still free to enter and enjoy.

Cross Gower Street to Montague Place, which runs along the rear of the vast **British Museum** ❸ (see box, above). On the left, next to Malet Street Gardens, is one of the city's most striking buildings, Art Deco **Senate House** ❹ (Grade II* listed), designed by British architect Charles Holden (1875-1960) and constructed between 1933 and 1936. It's the administrative centre of the University of London – the university's first permanent home – and houses the Senate House Library, one

Bedford Square

Cabmen's Shelters

Established throughout London for hansom cab drivers in the 19th century, these shelters were intended as an alcohol-free alternative to pubs where cabbies invariably took refuge in inclement weather (any excuse), with inevitable consequences! There are 12 shelters remaining in London, all Grade II listed, and they still provide refreshments to licensed cabbies.

of the world's largest humanities collections.

At the end of Montague Place is **Russell Square ⑤** (7.30am-10pm). One of London's busiest squares, its gardens are large enough to escape most of the surrounding road noise – and there's also a café. The square was laid out in 1800 by Humphry Repton for Francis Russell, 5th Duke of Bedford, whose statue stands in solitary splendour at the southern end. On the northeast side is the magnificent **Principal London ⑥** hotel – formerly the Hotel Russell – built in 1898 by the architect Charles Fitzroy Doll. Its striking façade is clad in decorative thé-au-lait ('tea

with milk') terracotta based on the Chateau de Madrid on the Bois de Boulogne in Paris. The hotel features colonnaded balconies, cherubs and four figures above the main entrance, representing the four Protestant English Queens: Elizabeth I, Mary II, Anne and Victoria.

Turn right at the end of Montague Place and enter the square from the south; walk to the centre and take the left-hand path to the exit in the western corner. Note the green **Cabmen's Shelter ⑦** (see box, left). Cross over diagonally to Thornhaugh Street, home to the School of Oriental and African Studies (SOAS). On the left-hand corner is the SOAS's free **Brunei Gallery ⑧** (Tue-Sat 10.30am-5pm), which has a delightful Japanese roof garden.

Continue up Thornhaugh Street to **Woburn Square ⑨** (8am to 8pm or dusk), the smallest of Bloomsbury's squares. Designed by Thomas Cubitt and built between 1829 and 1847, it's named after Woburn Abbey, the main country seat of the Dukes of Bedford. Woburn Square leads into **Gordon Square ⑩** (8am to

The Principal London

8pm or dusk), named for the 6th Duke of Bedford's second wife, Lady Georgina Gordon. As you stroll through the square take a detour to the southwest corner where there's an area of woodland flora, including bluebells, cow parsley and dog violets.

Leave by the eastern exit onto Gordon Square (the road) and turn right onto Endsleigh Place and right again to **Tavistock Square**  . Dating from 1825, this is one of the green hearts of Bloomsbury and its layout of London planes and lawns is typical of many city squares. What sets it apart is the large number of memorials, which include a bronze of Mahatma Gandhi, and busts of writer Virginia Woolf (who lived at number 52, destroyed in World War Two) and Dame Louisa Aldrich-Blake, one of the UK's first female surgeons. There's also a cherry tree planted in memory of the victims of the Hiroshima nuclear bomb. Leave the square on the eastern side and turn left to follow Tavistock Square into Upper Woburn Place, with the British

Woburn Walk

Medical Association building on your right. Take the first right into **Woburn Walk** ⑫ (see box, below), a delightful pedestrianised street. There's a blue plaque on one of the houses in the block numbered 1-7, recalling that the poet W. B. Yeats lived there from 1895-1919.

At the end is Duke's Road which has another run of Cubitt's bow-fronted shops and, on the right, The Place Theatre with its attractive terracotta façade; look above the door for the medallion of Mars and Minerva by Thomas Brock, the insignia of the 20th Middlesex Rifle Volunteers. Retrace your steps and turn right into Burton Street, then left into Burton Place to **Cartwright Gardens** ⑬ . The crescent-shaped gardens were built between 1809 and 1811 and were named in honour of local resident and political reformer John Cartwright (1740-1824); there's a bronze statue of him by George Clarke in the gardens.

Woburn Walk

An elegant paved pedestrian thoroughfare, Woburn Walk's entrance is tucked away between the Number Twelve restaurant and the County Hotel on Upper Woburn Place. Designed by Thomas Cubitt in 1822 as a shopping street, both sides of the walk have attractive low terraces of well-preserved, bow-fronted shops, painted black at ground-floor level and cream above. Antiquated street lamps add to the character of the walkway, which is decidedly Dickensian.

Food & Drink

1 **Store Street Espresso:** A handsome, minimalist coffee shop with plenty of seating and delicious food (Mon-Fri 7.30am-7pm, Sat 9am-6pm, Sun 10am-5pm, £).

14 **Fork Deli Patisserie:** Friendly café offering a good selection of cakes and pastries baked on site (Mon-Fri 7.30am-7pm, Sat 8.30am-4pm, Sun 9am-4pm, £).

22 **Lamb:** Lovely Victorian pub serving excellent Young's ales and traditional pub grub (11am-11pm/midnight, £).

29 **London Review Cake Shop:** A modern literary teahouse with an irresistible choice of cakes (10am-6.30pm, closed Sun, £).

Russell, a traditional pub named after a two-time, 19th-century Prime Minister and grandfather of Bertrand Russell. Just past the pub is the **Fork Deli Patisserie** 14 , a friendly café/coffee shop/patisserie/deli, well worth a stop.

Continuing along Marchmont Street, cross over Tavistock Place and around 200m further, on the left, is the **Brunswick Centre** 15 , a '60s Modernist building housing residential units alongside an eclectic mix of fashion, dining and entertainment options, including

Foundling Museum

One of London's most poignant collections, the museum tells the story of the Foundling Hospital, London's first home for abandoned children. It involved three major figures in British history: philanthropist Sir Thomas Coram (1668-1751), artist William Hogarth (1697-1764) and composer George Frederic Handel (1685-1759). Coram founded the Hospital after being appalled by the number of abandoned children living on London's streets. The museum's collection charts the history of the Foundling Hospital, from its foundation in 1739 to its closure in 1954. The museum was also Britain's first public art gallery and exhibits paintings and sculptures donated by Hogarth, Thomas Gainsborough, Joshua Reynolds and others.

The gardens (enclosed by iron railings) mainly consist of mature plane trees and lawn, along with residents' tennis courts.

Walk around the gardens to the right, passing a series of original Georgian buildings now housing hotels, to reach Marchmont Street. Almost immediately on the right (nos 91-3) is the Lord John

a state-of-the-art Curzon art-house cinema (the entrance is on Bernard Street). Turn left at the end of Marchmont Street and walk along the southern perimeter of the Brunswick Centre, turning left again into Brunswick Square and **Brunswick Square Gardens** ⑯ (dawn to dusk) – all were named after Caroline of Brunswick, wife to the Prince Regent, later George IV. Near the centre of the gardens is the Brunswick Plane, nominated in 2008 as one of the Great Trees of London by the tree-planting charity, Trees for Cities.

Walk up the western side of the square into Hunter Street, then turn right into Handel Street and continue straight ahead into beautiful **St George's Gardens** ⑰ . They occupy what was once the burial ground for two nearby churches – St George's Bloomsbury and St George the Martyr (now St George's Holborn) in Queen Square – and were where the first recorded case of body-snatching took place in 1777. Exit the gardens via the footpath in the southwest corner to the **Foundling Museum** ⑱ (see box, left).

Leaving the museum via Brunswick Square, enter the gardens and walk along the eastern path and exit in the southeast corner. Go straight ahead down Lansdowne Terrace and turn left on Guilford Street and right on Guilford Place. Opposite is **Coram's Fields** ⑲ (7

Sicilian Avenue

Sicilian Avenue is one of Bloomsbury's most charming streets and an oasis of calm, so-named due to its authentic southern Italian feel, screened at both ends by Ionic columns and lined with Corinthian columns. Designed by Robert James Worley as a pedestrianised shopping street and built between 1906 and 1910, it was the inspiration of Herbrand Arthur Russell, 11th Duke of Bedford, who travelled to Sicily in the early 20th century. The avenue boasts beautiful architecture with ornate carved stone façades, the walkways edged in Sicilian black and white marble, while down the centre are lamp standards and parasols.

acres/2.8ha), the city's first public children's playground, which pays tribute to the founder of the Foundling Hospital. Adults – defined as anyone over the age of 16 – are only permitted entry when accompanied by a child aged 15 or under. Guilford Place merges

Lamb's Conduit Street

into Bloomsbury's most elegant and famous shopping street, **Lamb's Conduit Street** ⑳, which takes its name from a wealthy Tudor gentleman, William Lambe, who built a conduit (or pipe) here to supply the city with spring water. On the right is the sprawling **Great Ormond Street Hospital** ㉑ for children, created in response to the shocking child mortality rate in the mid-19th century, when only half of all babies born into poverty reached their first birthday.

Today, Lamb's Conduit Street is home to a wealth of boutiques and splendid pubs, cafés and restaurants. If you fancy a pint, try the **Lamb** ㉒ at number 94 – built in 1729 but later remodelled – a fine example of Victorian design, including etched glass, a central horseshoe bar and snob screens to protect drinkers' privacy. It dates from a time when actors and music hall stars were regulars, and pictures of them adorn the walls. Charles Dickens used to sup here when he lived in nearby Doughty Street (his former home at number 48 is now the Charles Dickens Museum).

St George's Bloomsbury

At the end of Lamb's Conduit Street cross Theobalds Road into Red Lion Street and after a few metres bear right down Lamb's Conduit Passage, which leads to **Conway Hall** ㉓. The HQ of the Conway Hall Ethical Society – thought to be the oldest surviving free-thought organisation in the world – the hall plays host to a wide variety of events, from conferences and lectures to concerts and conventions. It overlooks **Red Lion Square Gardens** ㉔, laid out in 1684 by Nicholas Barbon (nos 14 to 17 are original houses, re-fronted in the 19th century). The gardens contain a number of statues, including one of politician Fenner Brockway and a bust of Bertrand Russell. From the gardens take Fisher Street and cross Southampton Row to **Sicilian Avenue** ㉕ (see box, page 35).

At the end of the avenue turn left into Bloomsbury Way, opposite **Bloomsbury Square Garden** ㉖ (7.30am-dusk), one of London's earliest squares, developed by the 4th Earl of Southampton in the 1660s to complement his mansion. The house has long gone but the gardens still reflect some of Humphry Repton's early 19th-century design of lawns, shrubberies and statuesque trees. Continue for 100m past Bury Place to **St George's Bloomsbury** ㉗, a Grade I listed English Baroque church. Built 1716-1731 and designed by Nicholas Hawksmoor (1661-1736), pupil and former assistant to Sir Christopher Wren, it's the architect's most idiosyncratic work. It's topped by London's most eccentric spire, stepped like a pyramid and crowned by a statue of George I in Roman dress posing as St George.

Just past the church turn right into Museum Street and left down Little Russell Street; on your right is the unique **Cartoon Museum** ㉘ , dedicated to preserving the best of British cartoons, caricatures, comics and animation, from the 18th century to the present day. Turn around, retrace your steps across Museum Street and along Little Russell Street, turning left at the end into Bury Place. A few steps along on the right you'll see the **London Review Bookshop** ㉙ (see box).

London Review Bookshop

Owned by venerable publication, *London Review of Books* (www.lrb. co.uk), this is one of London's most distinctive independent bookshops, an attractive space with a lovely ambience. Tucked inside is one of the city's most popular cafés, the London Review Cake Shop.

Turn right at the end of Bury Place into Great Russell Street and the top end of Bloomsbury Square, and left at the end onto Southampton Row. After around 200m turn right into Cosmo Place to **Queen Square** ㉚ (7.30am to dusk), named in honour of Queen Anne (1665-1714). Dating from around 1716, the square is a shady rectangle with a variety of trees, roses and bedding displays. Look for the sculpture of Sam the cat, perched on a wall – a feline memorial to champion of local causes, Patricia Penn. On the corner of Cosmo Place is the Queen's Larder, an intimate pub where, legend has it, Queen Charlotte (wife of George III) stored food for the king in the cellar when she was treating his illness in a nearby house. Opposite is St George's Holborn (also called St George the Martyr), built in 1703–06 by Arthur Tooley; it was once known as the sweeps' church, as parishioners provided Christmas dinners for 100 chimney sweeps' apprentices or 'climbing boys'.

Walk around the square to the northeast corner and exit via Queen Anne's Walk onto Guilford Street, where you turn left. After around 100m, turn right into Herbrand Street and on the first right-hand corner is the **Horse Hospital** ㉛ , an original example of a two-floor, purpose-built stable and infirmary where hansom cab horses were treated. It's now an alternative and experimental arts venue encompassing art, film, fashion, literature and music. Opposite is the cosy 18th-century **Friend at Hand** ㉜ pub, your 'last chance' saloon on this walk, which terminates around the corner from Herbrand Street at Russell Square tube station.

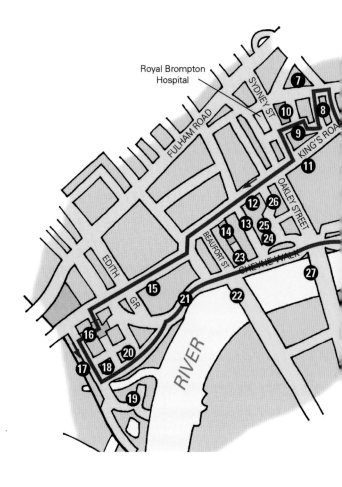

Royal Brompton Hospital

SYDNEY ST

FULHAM ROAD

KING'S ROAD

OAKLEY STREET

BEAUFORT ST

CHEYNE WALK

EDITH GR

RIVER

1 Sloane Square
2 Peter Jones
3 King's Road
4 ⬤ Saatchi Gallery
5 Partridge's Store
6 Bywater Street
7 Chelsea Common
8 Godfrey Street
9 Builder's Arms
10 St Luke's
11 Chelsea Old Town Hall
12 Oka

⬤ Places of Interest   ⬤ Food & Drink

START & END
Sloane Square

CHELSEA BRIDGE ROAD

CHELSEA EMBANKMENT

THAMES

BATTERSEA PARK

Chelsea

Distance: 4 miles (6½ km)
Terrain: easy, flat terrain
Duration: 2 hours
Start/End: Sloane Square tube
Postcode: SW1W 8BB

Chelsea is one of London's wealthiest and most fashionable areas, long the haunt of London's movers and shakers, from artists to rock stars to fashionistas. It's even spawned its own reality TV show, Channel 4's *Made in Chelsea*, which 'stars' the affluent young hipsters of SW3. This quirky quarter of west London is bounded to the south by the Thames, to the west by Chelsea Harbour and Brompton Cemetery, to the east by Chelsea Bridge Road and Sloane Street, and to the north by Old Brompton Road and South Kensington. The manor of Chelsea pre-dates the *Domesday Book* of 1086; its name in Old English – Chelceth, Chelchith or Chelsey – meant 'landing place (on the river) for chalk or limestone'.

Although the riverside has long been a popular retreat – Henry VIII had a manor house here – Chelsea was a rural backwater until the 1800s. It began to attract the rich and famous in the 19th century and has been doing so ever since. Artists, writers and musicians came first, followed by film stars, models and fashion designers (and many Americans – it has one of the largest US expat communities in London). Chelsea – and King's Road in particular – played a prominent role in the Swinging Sixties, a term coined by *Time* magazine to describe the blossoming music, fashion and cultural scene happening in the city in the 1960s.

Chelsea used to be London's bohemian village – or villages, as the area encompasses a number of such settlements. To explore its streets, mews and squares is to walk in the footsteps of a host of colourful and famous figures, both past and present, many remembered by blue plaques.

Our walk takes you from Sloane Square along King's Road, with excursions around some of the area's most historic streets, visiting Chelsea Common and St Luke's Gardens, then heading to World's End at the

Chelsea

western fringes of Chelsea. From here we dip a toe into Chelsea Harbour and return to Sloane Square via the Thames Embankment and the glorious Royal Hospital, venue of the annual Chelsea Flower Show.

Start Walking…

Exit Sloane Square tube station and cross over Holbein Place to **Sloane Square 1** . Designed in 1771, it's named after Sir Hans Sloane (1660-1753), Lord of the manor of Chelsea, whose private collection provided the foundation for the British Museum. In the early '80s the square gave its name to the 'Sloane Rangers': ostentatiously well-off younger members of the upper classes. Today, it's famous as the location of **Peter Jones 2** department store and the delightful Royal Court Theatre.

Walk along the southern edge of the square and enter **King's Road 3** (see box, below), with Peter Jones on your right. A bit

Peter Jones

further along on the left is Duke of York Square, home to the **Saatchi Gallery 4** , one of London's foremost contemporary art galleries. Founded by advertising guru Charles Saatchi in 1985 to exhibit his private collection of contemporary art, the gallery is now housed (since 2008) in the former Duke of York's Headquarters, built in 1801 and now Grade II* listed. It has a nice café, the Gallery Mess, which is a good place for a caffeine shot to kick-start your day. Just past the gallery is **Partridge's Store 5** , one of the city's poshest grocers, with a royal warrant. On Saturdays, Partridge's Food Market is held on the square, offering a wide range of artisan produce from around 70 stalls.

Continue along King's Road, where after 200m you come to **Bywater Street 6** on the right, well worth a detour to view some

King's Road

Until 1830 this was literally 'the king's road', a private road built in 1694 for Charles II (and his cronies – who were given a special copper token with the king's head on it), linking St James's Palace with Hampton and Kew. Today, it's Chelsea's 'high street', extending for 2 miles (3.2km) from Sloane Square to the border with Fulham. In its ('60s) heyday it was the epicentre of London's fashion and music scene, but today – while still stylish – it's more often associated with the independent boutiques frequented by ageing Sloane Rangers and the *Made in Chelsea* cast.

Bywater Street

Walk 4

Godfrey Street

pretty pastel-hued terraces. Back on King's Road, take a right down Markham Street (opposite Marks & Spencer) and turn left on Cale Street at the end. Opposite is **Chelsea Common 7**, the last remaining section of the original common that almost disappeared under building work in the 19th century; it now comprises a neat garden area with flowering cherry trees and annual flowerbeds. The area around the green is its own little village, with a good range of independent shops and restaurants.

Swing left just past the green into **Godfrey Street 8**, one of the capital's prettiest neighbourhoods, boasting rows of colourful artisans' cottages – a very desirable address. At the end of the street turn right into Burnsall Street, right again to Astell Street and left into Britten Street. Here, on the left, is the **Builders Arms 9**, a popular gastropub occupying a three-storey Georgian building; its workaday name belies a stylish interior and upmarket menu (no sweet tea and doorstop sarnies here). Further along on the right is some of the tiniest houses in Chelsea (number 20) and **St Luke's 10** church (see box, left) and its glorious gardens, next to the Royal Brompton Hospital.

From the gardens turn left down Sydney Street where, after around 150m, you find yourself back on King's Road. Opposite is **Chelsea Old Town Hall 11**, an elegant Victorian Neo-Classical building. It's well-known as a hip registry office, where Chelsea's glitterati come to get spliced, although it also hosts an eclectic mix of social, artistic, retail and musical events. Just past the town hall is the Ivy Chelsea Garden restaurant – one of the spin-offs of the illustrious Ivy in Covent Garden. There's also a wealth of cheaper eateries here for the hoi polloi, including a branch of Pan-Asian and sushi chain **Oka 12**, some 300m up on the left opposite beautiful Carlyle Square, named after writer Thomas Carlyle, who

St Luke's Church

Grade I listed, St Luke's was built in 1824 to cater to an expanding congregation which had outgrown its parish church (now Chelsea Old Church).

Designed by James Savage (1799-1852), St Luke's has flying buttresses and Gothic perpendicular towers, and is almost the size of a cathedral (seating 2,500). It has associations with many famous people, not least Charles Dickens who married Catherine Hogarth here in 1836. The large burial ground was converted into a public garden in 1881 and is now noted for its beautiful flowerbeds and magnificent trees.

lived in Chelsea (see below). Just past the square is **Old Church Street** ⑬ , Chelsea's oldest throughfare which links Chelsea Embankment to Fulham Road. It's named after the Chelsea Old Church (All Saints) – at the Chelsea Embankment end of the street – and is mentioned as far back as 1566, when it was the more modest Church Lane. The street contains many lovely old buildings and is a visual treat.

The next turning on the left is **Paultons Square** ⑭ , a lovely garden square popular with writers. It was built 1836-40 on the site of a former market garden, land previously owned by Sir Thomas More and Sir Thomas Danvers (one of the signatories of the death warrant of Charles I.)

Soon after, the road winds to the left towards the river in an area known as **World's End** ⑮ . It got its name from James II, who would regularly ride down King's Road and considered it to be 'the end of the world'. It's still the less fashionable end of Chelsea, though its Victorian slums were replaced by council housing in the 20th century.

Food & Drink

④ **Gallery Mess:** The Saatchi Gallery's café is a good choice for morning coffee or a tasty lunch (10am-11.30pm, Sun 7pm, £).

⑨ **The Builders Arms:** Stylish gastropub in Britten Street with good beer and fine wines (noon-11pm/midnight, £-££).

⑫ **Oka:** A cosy restaurant on King's Road (number 251) offering a modern take on traditional Pan-Asian & sushi cuisines, eat-in or take away (noon-10.30pm, £).

⑱ **Lots Road Pub & Dining Room:** A handsome pub offering modern British cuisine and an exceptional range of beers (noon-10pm, Sun 9pm, £-££).

Lots Road Auctions

Around 100m past Ashburnham Road, turn left down Thorndike Close to **Westfield Park** ⑯ ,

a lovely neighbourhood park with lawns, trees, shrubs and flowerbeds (and toilets!). Cut west across the park, crossing Tetcott Road, to reach Lots Road. Turn left, where at no 71-73, is **Lots Road Auctions** ⑰ , made famous in recent years by Channel 4's fly-on-the-wall TV documentary *The Auction House*. Further down (at no 11) is **Lots Road Pub &**

Dining Room 18 , a handsome gastropub offering a wide range of craft and bottled beers. If you go straight ahead from the pub you cross a bridge over Chelsea Creek leading to **Chelsea Harbour** 19 , a luxury development on the Thames, Chelsea Harbour Pier (ferries to central London) and Imperial Wharf railway station.

Lots Road continues on the left and some 200m past the pub is the **606 Club** 20 , an intimate jazz club and restaurant offering live music seven nights a week. Carry on past Cremorne Gardens and bear right along Cremorne Road which, after around 200m, becomes **Cheyne Walk** 21 (see box, right), one of Chelsea's most prestigious addresses, with houseboats docked along the Thames. The next bridge along is **Battersea Bridge** 22 , designed by the prolific Victorian engineer Sir Joseph Bazalgette and opened in 1890; it's an arch bridge with five spans, and at just 40ft (12m) wide is the narrowest road bridge still spanning the river.

Just past Battersea Bridge is red-brick **Crosby Hall** 23 , the surviving part of a mansion built in 1466-75 for Sir John Crosby, a wealthy wool merchant. What makes it really remarkable is that the building was moved stone-by-stone from Bishopsgate to Chelsea in 1910 to rescue it from demolition. Next to the hall

is Danvers Street, where Sir Alexander Fleming (1881-1955), who discovered penicillin, lived at number 20.

Next to Danvers Street is Ropers Gardens, a small sunken garden with a fine nude statue – The Awakening by Gilbert Ledward (1915) – and just across Old Church Street there's another small garden surrounding a garish statue of **Sir Thomas More** ㉔ (1478-1535); a seated bronze by L. Cubitt Bevis (1969), with black robes and golden face and hands. More was a philosopher, theologian and statesman (Lord Chancellor) under Henry VIII – a risky business! He opposed Henry's Reformation and paid the price by losing his head. In happier days, More lived at nearby Beaufort House and was said to have 'put Chelsea on the map'.

Thomas Carlyle's House

More's statue sits in front of **Chelsea Old Church** ㉕, aka All Saints, formerly the parish church of Chelsea with parts dating from 1157. The handsome church is the only one in London to retain a chained library (albeit a small one), a curious throwback to medieval times, and it also boasts what's said to be London's second-finest collection of church monuments after Westminster Abbey.

Just past the church turn slightly inland on Cheyne Walk passing Cheyne Walk Brasserie at number 50. Immediately past the restaurant turn left into Cheyne Row, one of London's best-preserved early 18th-century streets, where at number 24 is **Thomas Carlyle's House** ㉖ (Wed-Sun 11am-5pm). Thomas and Jane Carlyle were a celebrated literary couple of their day; historian, philosopher and satirist, Thomas was one of the Victorian era's greatest writers, said to have inspired Charles Dickens, while his wife was a woman of letters and a renowned hostess. Their house, a beautiful Queen Anne property (1708), provides a fascinating insight into what life was

Albert Bridge

Designed by Rowland Mason Ordish and opened in 1873, Albert Bridge was originally a toll bridge. It wasn't much of an earner and after six years the tolls were scrapped; the tollbooths remain in place and are the only surviving examples in London. The bridge was nicknamed 'The Trembling Lady' due to its tendency to vibrate when large numbers of people walked over it – signs at the entrances warn 'troops must break step when marching over this bridge'! It looks particularly stunning at night, when it's illuminated.

like in the home of an educated middle-class Victorian couple.

Return to Cheyne Walk and continue for 200m to Oakley Street and **Albert Bridge** ㉗ (see box, page 45), named after Prince Albert, and Cadogan Pier from where Thames Clipper (ferry) boats run to central London and Canary Wharf. In front of the bridge are Albert Bridge Gardens, a small public park.

Chelsea Physic Garden

The 3½ acre (1.4ha) garden is a historic living museum, as well as a haven of beauty and relaxation, with a lovely café called Tangerine Dream (closed Saturdays). Founded in 1673, it's London's oldest botanical garden and Britain's second-oldest after one at the University of Oxford (founded 1621). Physic gardens grew plants and herbs for medicinal use and Chelsea is still used as a resource today by medical students. Note, however, that there's a high entrance fee, which must also be paid simply to access the café. The entrance is in Swan Walk. (See www.chelseaphysicgarden.co.uk for information.)

Crossing over Oakley Street, continue along the Chelsea Embankment to the final section of Cheyne Walk, where numbers 19-26 occupy what was once the site of Henry VIII's Manor House, and retain intriguing traces of the former buildings. In front of the walk – on either side of Oakley Street – are Chelsea Embankment Gardens, consisting of two strips of land with lovely ornamental bedding and shrubs, paths, seating and a number of statues and memorials. At the end of Cheyne Walk, turn left onto Royal Hospital Road, where on the right is the **Chelsea Physic Garden** ㉘ (see box, left), a 'secret' botanical garden founded in 1673.

A few hundred metres further up, on the right, is the **National Army Museum** ㉙ (free entry, daily 10am-5.30pm, www.nam. ac.uk). Look for the small section of the Berlin Wall on display just before the museum. The collection covers the period from 1066 to the present day, with exhibitions divided into different eras. Especially interesting and poignant are some of the personal accounts by soldiers, their families and the citizens of war-torn countries. Just after the museum, on your right is one of London's most magnificent buildings: the **Royal Hospital, Chelsea** ㉚ (see box, right). It occupies 52 acres (21ha) of grounds, including Ranelagh Gardens, contains over 500 mature trees and is the venue for the Chelsea Flower Show in May.

Just after the museum, turn left at the junction with Chelsea Bridge Road, and walk up to Sloane Square – from where you started – and the end of this walk.

Royal Hospital, Chelsea

The Royal Hospital for veteran soldiers was founded in 1682 by Charles II and designed by Sir Christopher Wren. It's built around three courtyards, the central one opening to the south, with side courtyards to the east and west. The building remains almost unchanged from Wren's original, except for minor alterations by Robert Adam between 1765 and 1782, and the stables, which were added by Sir John Soane in 1814. Today, the hospital is home to around 400 ex-army pensioners, who receive free board, lodging, nursing care and a distinctive red uniform. Much of the site is open to visitors, including the great hall, octagon, chapel, courtyards and grounds. There's also a small museum dedicated to the hospital's history. (See www.chelsea-pensioners.co.uk for more information.)

Chelsea Pensioners

Chapel

Royal Hospital, Chelsea

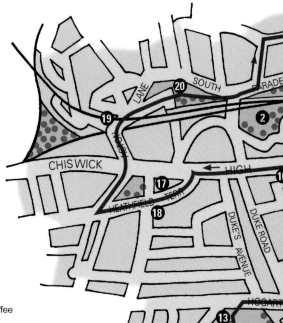

1. Chief Coffee
2. Chiswick Common
3. Old Cinema
4. Roebuck
5. Fuller's Brewery
6. Chiswick Mall
7. Church Street
8. St Nicholas Church
9. Powell's Walk
10. Chiswick House & Gardens
11. Chiswick House Café
12. Ionic Temple
13. Will to Win Tennis Club
14. Hogarth's House
15. La Trompette
16. George IV
17. Christ Church
18. Chiswick Town Hall
19. Chiswick Park Tube Station
20. Acton Green Common
21. St Michael and All Angels
22. The Tabard

● Places of Interest   ● Food & Drink

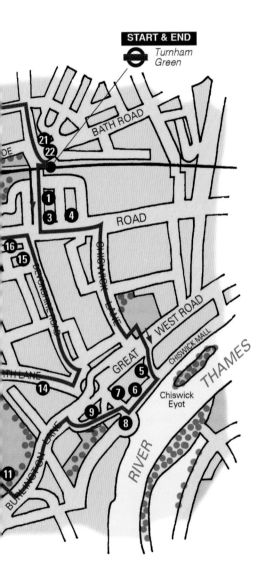

START & END
Turnham
Green

BATH ROAD

ROAD

WEST ROAD

CHISWICK MALL

THAMES

Chiswick
Eyot

GREAT

RIVER

DEVONSHIRE ROAD

CHISWICK LANE

BURLINGTON LANE

WALK 5

Chiswick

Distance: 4½ miles (7 km)
Terrain: easy, some moderate hills
Duration: 2½ hours
Start/End: Turnham Green tube
Postcode: W4 1QN

CHISWICK

The affluent west London suburb of Chiswick sits on a meander of the River Thames, with Kew to the west and Hammersmith to the east. It's first mentioned in around 1,000AD as Ceswican, which is reputedly Old English for 'cheese farm' and may derive from the annual cheese fair held here until the 18th century. Until the early 19th century it was a rural outpost relying on agriculture and fishing, and a popular country retreat from London; Chiswick House was where the Earls of Burlington escaped Piccadilly's heat in summer.

Now within the borough of Hounslow, Chiswick was originally part of the county of Middlesex (abolished in 1965) and grew out of four villages – Strand-on-the-Green on the river, Little Sutton to the east, Turnham Green to the northeast and Chiswick itself – which gradually merged. The area began to develop into a London suburb during the late 1800s and the population increased tenfold during the 19th century. Today, it's an attractive and sought-after place to live for its large period houses (a mixture of Georgian, Victorian and Edwardian), profusion of green spaces, proximity to the Thames and good transport links – not to mention its excellent range of shops (foodie heaven!), restaurants, pubs and cafés. It has also managed to retain its village atmosphere, notably around Bedford Park, Church Street and Turnham Green.

Our walk takes you from Chiswick Common along Chiswick High Road and down to the river at Chiswick Mall, then on to old Chiswick village and Chiswick House, continuing to Turnham Green and finishing in Bedford Park.

Start Walking…

Step out of Turnham Green tube station and turn left under the bridge. If you fancy a coffee to nudge you on your way, try **Chief Coffee** ❶ around 100m past the tube station, and left down Turnham Green Mews (next to Snap Dragon toy shop), which has a pinball lounge in the basement. Opposite is **Chiswick Common** ❷ (8.6 acres/3.5ha), once part of the Bishop of London's manor of Fulham, and a pastoral retreat until the mid-19th century. Today, the common is mainly grass, criss-crossed by paths, with mature trees around the perimeter, and is home to the Rocks Lane Multi Sport centre and a playground. Carry on down Turnham Green Terrace, which leads to Chiswick High Road. The terrace is one of Chiswick's premier shopping streets, featuring a welcome preponderance of independent shops, cafés and restaurants, including the outstanding Foubert's – super ice cream – and Charlotte's Bistro.

At the end of the Terrace, turn left onto bustling Chiswick High Road (see box, above). A short way along on the left is the **Old Cinema** ❸, a former Edwardian picture palace that's now a vast 'antique, vintage, and retro department store' (well worth a look). Around 100m further along

> ### Chiswick High Road
>
> The sprawling High Road – which runs for 1½ miles (2.5km) from Gunnersbury to Stamford Brook – is a hive of activity, dotted with leafy green spaces and upmarket high street chains, along with plenty of thriving independents. The wide pavements encourage an abundance of cafés, restaurants and pubs to provide outdoor seating on sunny days, giving the street a continental vibe.

is the **Roebuck** ❹ gastropub, on the corner with Thornton Avenue. It has a lovely beer garden, just the place to enjoy a large Sipsmith G&T (distilled in Chiswick) – or save it for a post-walk treat!

Chiswick Riverside

Around 50m past the Roebuck, cross the High Road and turn right down Chiswick Lane, lined with handsome Victorian houses. Around halfway down on the right, in Cranbrook Road, is the Sipsmith gin distillery (founded 2014), while a little further on is Homefield Recreation Ground, a popular sports venue. Just past the recreation ground cross over the

St Nicholas Church

The old village of Chiswick grew up around the church of St Nicholas, and the choice of saint testifies to the fact that Chiswick began as a fishing village: St Nicholas is the patron saint of fishermen and sailors, among others. The church's ragstone tower dates from 1446 and is the only reminder of the medieval church; the rest was rebuilt in 1882 by John Loughborough Pearson, one of Britain's leading Victorian architects.

Great West Road and head down Chiswick Lane South, passing **Fuller's Brewery** ❺ on the right, to Chiswick Mall. Beer has been brewed in Chiswick for over 350 years, although the brewery 'only' dates from 1845 (to book a tour see www.fullers.co.uk).

The **Chiswick Mall** ❻ – which is liable to flooding at high tide – runs along the River Thames from Church Street to Hammersmith, and is lined with large, attractive, mainly 18th-century, houses. The island in the Thames here is Chiswick Eyot – old English for a small island in a river or lake – which can be reached on foot at low tide. Note the draw (cargo) dock at the end of The Mall, the site of the ancient Chiswick ferry. Turn right along The Mall and stroll along the river to **Church Street** ❼ which swings inland. This was the heart of Old

Chiswick and still resembles a village high street with lovely old buildings, some of which were once pubs (such as The Old Burlington on the right, dating from the 15th century). A little further on, also on the right, is the former Lamb's Brewery, which operated from 1790 to the 1950s and now houses offices.

The main landmark here is **St Nicholas Church** ❽ (see box, left), a Perpendicular-style building with a shady churchyard and some illustrious residents; the graveyard is the last resting place of William Hogarth (1697-1764), fellow artist James McNeill Whistler (1834-1903), architect William Kent (1685-1748) and Frederick Hitch (1856-1913), who won a Victoria Cross for his bravery at the Battle of Rorke's Drift in South

Chiswick House

Built in 1727-9 and one of the finest examples of Palladian architecture in Britain, the design of Chiswick House (Fri-Wed, Apr-Nov, 10am-5/6pm, entrance fee) echoes that of classical temples. It's the result of a collaboration between the 3rd Earl of Burlington (1694-1753) – inspired by architecture he saw during his grand tours of Italy – and architect William Kent (1685-1748). (See http://chiswickhouseandgardens.org.uk for more information.)

Africa during the Anglo-Zulu War of 1879.

Just past the church go left down **Powell's Walk** ❾, an ancient right-of-way with high walls obscuring Chiswick's old cemetery. At the end turn left along Burlington Lane and follow the road round past St Mary's Convent (1910) on the corner of Corney Road. Opposite is the main entrance to **Chiswick House & Gardens** ❿. Go through the gateway, turn right onto Duke's Avenue and left (look for the blue sign) to Chiswick House (see box, left). The award-winning **Chiswick House Café** ⑪ on your right is recommended for lunch.

The 65 acres (26ha) of gardens – Grade I listed and recently restored at a cost of £12 million – are of huge historical significance as the birthplace of the English Landscape Movement; the style of sweeping elegance that replaced the earlier formality was the inspiration for great gardens from Blenheim Palace to New York's Central Park. The gardens were originally intended to resemble those of Ancient Rome, but were redesigned from the early 18th century in the geometrical style by Charles Bridgeman, to include ornamental buildings at the ends of vistas.

From the front of the house, follow the path to the left around the house to the gardens. When you're roughly in the middle of the gardens, with the **Ionic Temple** ⑫ and the lake on your left, take

the diagonal path to the northwest corner in the direction of the **Will to Win Tennis Club** ⑬. Exit via the path to the right of the tennis club which leads back to the Great West Road. Turn right, and around 250m along is **Hogarth's House** ⑭ (see box, above).

From the house continue east to the Hogarth Roundabout and Flyover (named after the great man – a dubious honour!) and cross via the underpass and walk up Devonshire Road. Once past Ingress Street, the attractive terraces give way to lifestyle and designer boutiques, galleries,

Hogath's House

Battle of Turnham Green

On 13th November 1642, Turnham Green was the venue for an important battle in the English Civil War. The Parliamentarians' front ran from modern South Parade to the garden walls of Chiswick House, while the Royalist army extended from Acton Green across Turnham Green and close to the line of Sutton Court Road. Although the battle resulted in a standoff, the Parliamentarians succeeded in blocking the Royalist army's way to London, and Charles I's army was forced to retreat to Oxford. The Civil War continued until 1646, but the Royalists never again approached London, which firmly supported the Parliamentarian cause. Thus the Battle of Turnham Green proved to have been decisive in ending the Royalists' hope of capturing London.

on the high road, dating from the late 18th century. Next door is the **George IV** ⑯, a Fuller's pub with a tranquil courtyard. After 300m or so you come to Turnham Green, a 'village green' with a fascinating history (see box, left). On the corner is the Chiswick War Memorial, while in the centre is lovely **Christ Church** ⑰ (1843), designed by Sir George Gilbert Scott. Turn left into Heathfield Terrace, which is lined with handsome period mansion blocks, and just past the church, opposite Town Hall Avenue, is **Chiswick Town Hall** ⑱, opened in 1901 and Grade II listed, though no longer a centre of local government.

Continue around the green, turn right along Sutton Lane North, and cross Chiswick High Road to Acton Lane; 200m further on is **Chiswick Park Tube Station** ⑲, with its attractive semi-circular (Grade II listed) ticket hall and, just over Bollo Road on the left, the entrance to the lovely Gunnersbury Triangle Nature Reserve. Turn right at the station, under the bridge, and when you reach **Acton Green Common** ⑳ bear right along Hardwicke Road. After a short distance enter the common and go straight ahead, cross over Fisher's Lane and walk along the northern fringe of Chiswick Common. Halfway along, cross South Parade and turn left along The Orchard.

This is Bedford Park, a conservation area – thought to be the world's first garden suburb – where many houses were designed by celebrated

restaurants and other businesses. On the left is the superb **La Trompette** ⑮, an award-winning restaurant serving modern French cuisine created by renowned chef Rob Weston.

Christ Church, Turnham Green

At the end of the road turn left along Chiswick High Road. Around 50m up on the left at number 183 is Foster Books, a delightful family-run bookshop (selling rare, collectors' editions) occupying the oldest shop building

architect Richard Norman Shaw in the 1870s. His houses have retained their picturesque red brick frontages and beautiful detailing, and line the streets to the east and north of South Parade. One particularly vocal resident was poet John Betjeman, who described Bedford Park as 'the most significant suburb built in the last century, probably the most significant in the western world'.

Walk up The Orchard, turn right into Bedford Road and take the second right onto The Avenue. Continue back to the common, where opposite is Grade II* listed **St Michael and All Angels 21**, a lovely Queen Anne Revival style church in red brick, designed by Norman Shaw and completed in 1892. Opposite the church in Bath Road is **The Tabard 22**, a unique Arts and Crafts pub built in 1880; on the first floor is the Tabard Theatre, a 96-seat fringe theatre run independently of the pub.

From here it's a short walk south down Turnham Green Terrace to reach Turnham Green tube station and your journey home.

Food & Drink

1. **Chief Coffee:** This café, just off Turnham Green Terrace, is a good place for a caffeine shot (8am-5.30pm, Sat 9am-6pm, Sun 10am 5.30pm, £).

4. **Roebuck:** A glorious gastropub on Chiswick High Road, and a good choice for a pint or a tasty lunch (11am/noon-11pm/midnight, £).

11. **Chiswick House Café:** Award-winning café in Chiswick Gardens offering a British seasonal menu (8.30am-4/6pm, £).

15. **La Trompette:** High-end modern French cuisine in a stylish contemporary space on Devonshire Road (booking essential, 020-8747 1836, noon-2.30pm, 6.30-10.30pm, ££-£££).

Bedford Park house

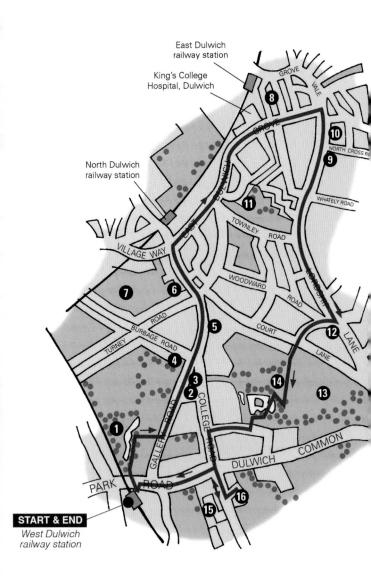

East Dulwich
railway station

King's College
Hospital, Dulwich

North Dulwich
railway station

GROVE VALE

GROVE

8

10

NORTH CROSS R

9

WHATELY ROAD

DULWICH

11

TOWNLEY   ROAD

VILLAGE WAY

EAST

7   **6**

ROAD

BURBAGE ROAD

WOODWARD

ROAD

LORDSHIP

TURNEY

5

COURT

12

LANE

4

LANE

3

2

COLLEGE   ROAD

14

13

1

GALLERY   ROAD

DULWICH   COMMON

PARK   ROAD

15   **16**

START & END

West Dulwich
railway station

● Places of Interest	● Food & Drink

WALK 6

Dulwich

Distance: 4½ miles (7 km)
Terrain: moderate, some hills
Duration: 2½ hours
Start/End: West Dulwich rail
Postcode: SE21 8SN

DULWICH

One of London's most attractive and unique areas, Dulwich is in the southeast of the capital, straddling the boroughs of Southwark and Lambeth. It's among the oldest settlements in London, and was first recorded as Dilwihs in a charter granted by King Edgar the Peaceful in 967AD; the name derives from the Old English words *dile wisc*, meaning 'dill meadow'. After the Norman Conquest the manor was granted by Henry I to the Priory of Bermondsey, which owned it through the Middle Ages until the dissolution of the monasteries, when it was seized by Henry VIII. The estate, which extended (as it does today) from Denmark Hill to what are now the Crystal Palace grounds on Sydenham Hill, passed to the Calton family in 1544 (there's an avenue in Dulwich named after them).

What makes Dulwich so special today is almost entirely due to one man, Edward Alleyn (see box opposite), who purchased the manor of Dulwich from Sir Francis Calton in 1605 and founded a school and almshouses for the poor; this was the forerunner of Dulwich College, around which Dulwich grew.

From the early 18th century onwards, the college allowed wealthy Londoners – often the parents of pupils – to build substantial houses in the area, thus maintaining the value and desirability of the estate. To this day, Dulwich Village remains part of the Dulwich Estate, which owns the freehold of around 1,500 acres (607ha) in the area, including a number of private roads and a tollgate.

Modern Dulwich consists of Dulwich Village, East Dulwich, West Dulwich and the Southwark half of Herne Hill. The village – a conservation area since 1968 – is one of the few inner London areas to maintain 'true' village charm, with lovely period architecture, abundant green spaces, unique independent shops and an enviable community spirit. Our walk explores the village and its surrounding areas, from West Dulwich via Belair Park to Dulwich Picture Gallery, along Dulwich Village to Lordship Lane, returning via Dulwich Park and College.

Start Walking…

Leaving West Dulwich railway station, turn right to walk under

---

Edward Alleyn

Edward ('Ned') Alleyn (1566-1626), a leading actor and a contemporary of Shakespeare, was the founder of Dulwich College and Alleyn's School. He retired from acting in 1598 at the height of his fame and went into business, with shares in several profitable playhouses (including the Rose Theatre), bear-pits and brothels in Southwark. In 1604 he was appointed Joint Master of the Royal Bears, Bulls and Mastiff Dogs, a lucrative post that made him extremely wealthy. Alleyn's connection with Dulwich began in 1605, when he bought the manor of Dulwich for the sum of £5,000. In 1619, he founded a charitable foundation, the College of God's Gift. He endowed it with his manor and other property and, since he had no children, it was the beneficiary of his entire estate. Some 400 years later the college is still a well-regarded independent school and the charity has evolved into the Dulwich Estate.

---

the bridge and cross the South Circular Road and enter **Belair Park** ❶ . Southwark's only Grade II* listed landscape, this beautiful park (26 acres/10.6ha) with lake, gardens and wildlife area, was once the grounds of Belair House, a country villa built in 1785 in the style of (or possibly by) Richard Adam. Follow the path around to the right, past the tennis courts to Belair House. The house is now a restaurant, wedding and events venue and its lodge, entrance gates and an old stable building are all Grade II listed.

Exit the park just past the house onto Gallery Road and look for the white gates of Lover's Walk opposite, a delightful path leading to College Road – one of Dulwich's most prestigious residential streets – through a grove of trees. Turn left at the end of the Walk, and around 150m up on the left is **Dulwich Picture Gallery** ❷ (see box, page 60), which has an impressive collection of Old Masters and is well worth a visit. It also has a wonderful café.

Old Dulwich College

Just past the gallery is the Old College of Dulwich Estate – the former school has been known as

Dulwich Picture Gallery

Designed by Sir John Soane (1753-1837) and opened in 1817, the majestic Dulwich Picture Gallery (Tue-Sun 10am to 5pm, closed Mon, entrance fee) was England's first purpose-built, public art gallery, and its design – large rooms flooded with natural light – proved highly influential in the way we design art galleries. The collection itself was largely bequeathed by art dealers Francis Bourgeois and Noel Deschamps, and was originally assembled for the King of Poland. The gallery houses one of the world's most important collections of European Old Masters from the 17th and18th centuries, including works by Canaletto, Constable, Gainsborough, Hogarth, Landseer, Murillo, Poussin, Raphael, Rembrandt, Reynolds, Rubens and Van Dyck.

the Old College since 1870, when the New College opened further south off College Road – one wing of which now houses the administrative offices of the estate. A statue of Edward Alleyn by Louise Simpson was unveiled here in 2005. Adjacent to the college is **Christ's Chapel of God's Gift at Dulwich** ❸, the first of Alleyn's Foundation buildings to be completed, consecrated by the Archbishop of Canterbury in 1616. The chapel has a splendid organ, built by George England in 1759, thought to be the oldest surviving example of this famous organ-builder's work. The adjacent almshouses (Edward Alleyn House) were originally constructed in 1613-1616 and are still in use today, although they're now located in the left wing of the Old College (when facing the chapel).

Exit onto Gallery Road and turn right, where (just before the end) is the Tudor-style **Old Grammar School** ❹ on the left, built by Sir Charles Barry in 1842 for 60 boys, which later moved to North Dulwich and became known as Alleyn's School. At the junction there's a distinctive old-fashioned fingerpost, one of many throughout the estate, and a red granite drinking fountain (1877) in memory of Dr George Webster, founder of the first British Medical Association, who worked in Dulwich as a GP.

Continue straight ahead on Dulwich Village, formerly the High Street, but renamed to ensure you know where you are! The road is lined with fine Georgian houses on the right-hand side, with white

Dulwich Picture Gallery

Lordship Lane

East Dulwich's oldest street, Lordship Lane (which even has its own website – www.lordshiplane. co.uk) was the border between the 'lordships' or manors of Camberwell-Friern and Dulwich Manor in the 17th century. The area was transformed from fields and market gardens into Victorian suburbs between 1865 and1885. Today, it has a cosy village atmosphere and is East Dulwich's main shopping (and 'foodie') street, with a wealth of interesting independent shops, restaurants, pubs and cafés.

chain posts enclosing grassed areas, a common sight throughout the estate. A few hundred metres down on the right is the splendid Italian restaurant Rocca, while next door is the imposing **Crown & Greyhound** 5 pub and boutique hotel. An iconic local landmark, the dog-friendly pub offers good ales and food (delicious Sunday roasts) and has a delightful beer garden.

A bit further along, on the right – at the junction with Calton Avenue – is a burial ground of the victims of plague in 17th-century Dulwich. Carry on over the crossroads – Dulwich Hamlet Junior School on the left is the venue for the **Dulwich Village Farmers' Market** 6 on Saturdays (10am-2pm) – and as you approach the top of Dulwich Village, over on your left is the Griffin Sports Club, owned and managed by King's College University (London), and beyond it

the **Herne Hill Velodrome** 7, built in 1891 and one of the oldest cycling tracks in the world.

Turn right onto East Dulwich Grove, past James Allen's Girls' School established in 1886. Around 600m further on turn left down Melbourne Grove, where at number 45 is the fascinating **House of Dreams** 8, a terraced house that's been transformed into the personal gallery/museum of artist, textile designer and art director Steven Wright. The mind-boggling museum is an absolute must for design creatives (see www.stephenwrightartist. com/contact.php for open days). Retrace your steps to East Dulwich Grove, turn left and a short distance further on you reach the junction with **Lordship Lane** 9 (see box, left), where you turn right.

Dulwich Village house

Lordship Lane offers an impressive choice of eateries and pubs. Our favourites – going from north to south – include the Brick House Bakery (licensed café), Franco Manca (best pizzas in town), MEATliquor East Dulwich (super burgers and cocktails),

Food & Drink

(2) Dulwich Picture Gallery Café: The superb gallery café offers a wide range of beverages and food, which can be enjoyed on the terrace or lawn (Tue-Sun, 8.30/9am-5pm, closed Mondays, £).

(5) Crown & Greyhound: Iconic gastropub (and hotel) in Dulwich Village, offering good ales and a large garden (noon-11pm, £).

(10) The Palmerston: A celebrated gastropub on Lordship Lane with an extensive wine list (Mon-Thu noon-11pm, Fri-Sun from 10am, £-££).

(14) Dulwich Clock Café: The café in Dulwich Park is a pleasant venue for coffee, tea or lunch (8am-4pm, £).

The Palmerston (10) – a superb award-winning gastropub – the East Dulwich Picturehouse & Café (cinema with a lovely café and garden), Oddono's (for scrumptious Italian ice cream) and Franklins (a landmark British restaurant). Suitably satiated, continue south to Townley Road (around 100m past the Lordship Pub) and turn right; around 400m up on the right is imposing **Alleyn's School (11)** – the descendant of the Old Grammar School on Gallery Road – established here as an independent boys' school in 1887.

Return to Lordship Lane, turn right and continue south for another 600m to its junction with Eynella Road, which is encircled by another cluster of shops and restaurants. On the corner is **Dulwich Library (12)**, a splendid Victorian building financed by philanthropist John Passmore Edwards (1823-1911), which opened in 1897. In the same year, the children's author, Enid Blyton was born above a shop on Lordship Lane (nos 352-6), which is marked with a blue plaque. Turn down Eynella Road, which leads to **Dulwich Park (13)** (see box, right), one of Greater London's green treasures.

On entering the park, continue straight ahead on the path dissecting the East and West Lawns and turn right at the cross paths to the **Dulwich Clock Café (14)**, a lovely spot to break your walk. Turn left past the café and cross the boating lake via the boardwalk and follow

Dulwich Park

Dulwich Park

Dulwich Park (72 acres/29ha, 8am to dusk) was formerly part of the manor of Dulwich; the land was donated in 1885 by the Dulwich Estates' Board of Governors to create a public park. Opened in 1890, it's considered to be the forerunner of modern country parks. The park is noted for its wildflower meadows, majestic oak trees, formal gardens, period buildings – including a café – boating lake and children's playground. If you're the sporty type, there are free tennis courts and table tennis tables, an outdoor gym, sports pitches and a bowling green.

the path south of the lake, exiting the park onto Frank Dixon Way – lined with beautiful detached period houses – just past the tennis courts. Continue to the right and turn left onto College Road, some 200m south of Dulwich Picture Gallery that you visited earlier. Carry on south, crossing the South Circular Road (Dulwich Common), and on the right is the impressive frontage of **Dulwich College** 15 . This independent day and boarding school for boys is the New College (after the Old College outgrew its site) and was built 1866-70 by Charles Barry Jnr – son of Sir Charles Barry, who designed Westminster Palace – and financed from the sale of land to the South Eastern and Chatham Railway Company.

On the left side of College Road, opposite the college, is a large pond – dug to provide clay for the production of tiles, bricks and chimney pots for the estate – while just beyond it are **Pond Cottages** 16 . The cottages housed the kilns and weren't originally intended for residential use. On the right just past the college is Blew House, which Alleyn owned, while some 300m further on is a toll gate built in 1789 at the entrace too the Dulwich Estate. This is London's last remaining toll house (£1.20 for vehicles, free for pedestrians), with a board listing the pre-decimalisation charges (it cost 2½ old pennies to take your hog for a walk). Return to the South Circular Road, and turn left along the perimeter of the college grounds to West Dulwich railway station and the end of the walk.

Dulwich College

1. Hand Made Food
2. Clarendon Hotel
3. The Paragon
4. St Michael & All Angels
5. Cator Estate
6. Blackheath Halls
7. The Crown

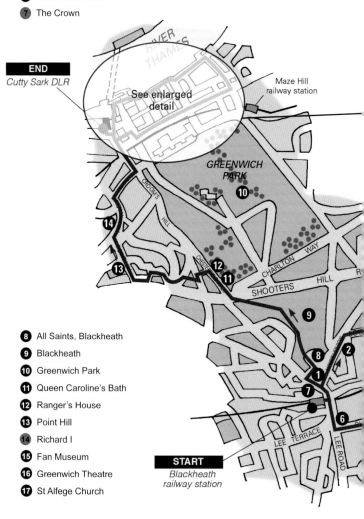

END
Cutty Sark DLR

See enlarged detail

Maze Hill railway station

GREENWICH PARK

CROOMS HILL

CHESTER

CHARLTON WAY

SHOOTERS HILL

R

LEE TERRACE

LEE ROAD

START
Blackheath railway station

8. All Saints, Blackheath
9. Blackheath
10. Greenwich Park
11. Queen Caroline's Bath
12. Ranger's House
13. Point Hill
14. Richard I
15. Fan Museum
16. Greenwich Theatre
17. St Alfege Church

● Places of Interest ● Food & Drink

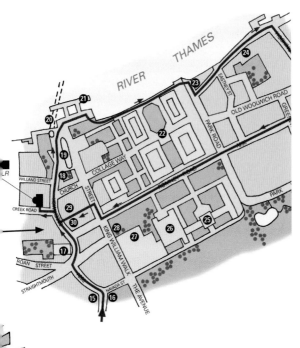

18 Gypsy Moth
19 Cutty Sark
20 Greenwich Foot Tunnel
21 Greenwich Pier
22 Old Royal Naval College
23 Trafalgar Tavern
24 Trinity Hospital
25 Queen's House
26 National Maritime Museum
27 De Vere Devonport House
28 Throne of Earthly Kings
29 Greenwich Market
30 Red Door Café & Gallery

Greenwich & Blackheath

> **Distance:** 5½ miles (9 km)
> **Terrain:** moderate, some hills
> **Duration:** 3 hours
> **Start:** Blackheath rail
> **End:** Cutty Sark DLR
> **Postcode:** SE3 9LE

L ocated in one of the greenest areas of southeast London, Greenwich and Blackheath are noted for their royal connections, charming architecture and sheer desirability. Greenwich is by far the older settlement, and has evidence of both Roman and Saxon occupation. Its name means either 'green village' in Anglo-Saxon or 'green reach' in old Norse. During the Middle Ages it was a fishing village, significant for its location on the River Thames, but it was in the 15th century, during the reign of Henry VII (1485-1509), that Greenwich gained real importance as a royal power base.

It was Henry VI's uncle, Humphrey, Duke of Gloucester, who first built a house at Greenwich in 1447. His manor house, Bella Court, later evolved into the Tudor Palace of Placentia, aka Greenwich Palace. This was the principal residence of Henry VII, and the birthplace of both Henry VIII and his two daughters, Mary I and Elizabeth I. It remained a royal palace for two centuries, but fell into disrepair during the Civil War. The last monarch to use Greenwich was James II. His daughter Mary donated the palace site to the Greenwich Hospital for sailors (1692-1869); this became the Royal Naval College, a training establishment from 1873 to 1998, and is now part of the Maritime Greenwich World Heritage Site.

The palace presence transformed Greenwich into a substantial resort town, popular with the aristocracy, and today it's a vibrant community with a wealth of beautiful Georgian and Victorian homes, and an abundance of independent shops, restaurants, cafés and pubs.

Separated from Greenwich Park by Shooters Hill Road, Blackheath takes its name from the windswept common, recorded in 1166 as Blachehedfeld ('dark

Greenwich & Blackheath

coloured heathland'). The village is comparatively new, having developed in the 1820s to cater for the middle classes moving into the area, and grown rapidly with the coming of the railways in 1849. Like Greenwich, it's one of south London's most desirable residential areas.

The walk takes us around **Blackheath Village and across the common, skirting the western edge of Greenwich Park, winding its way through the streets of West Greenwich before taking a tour of Greenwich, its riverfront and historic World Heritage Site.**

Start Walking…

Leaving Blackheath station, turn left along Blackheath Village (also the name of the road). Opposite where the road forks is **Hand Made Food ❶**, a good spot for breakfast or coffee to get you fired up. Take the right fork to Montpelier Vale, which is lined with a wealth of eateries and boutiques, and continue straight ahead on Montpelier Row. This is one of Blackheath's most prestigious addresses, lined with 18th-century townhouses – originally built for City merchants and seafarers – a number of which make up the imposing **Clarendon Hotel ❷**.

Blackheath was a massing point for Wat Tyler's Peasants' Revolt of 1381, a protest against the original poll tax, when 100,000 'rebels' gathered on the heath before their doomed 'assault' on London. A road on the western edge of the heath is named after Tyler who met a grisly end at Smithfield a month later.

Around 150m past the hotel is the Princess of Wales pub (named after Caroline of Brunswick, estranged wife of George IV), where you turn right into South Row – just across the road is the Prince of Wales pond on the heath. **The Paragon ❸**, a short way up on the right, is one of London's finest Georgian crescents, designed by Michael Searles and built in the 1790s. The Grade I listed crescent comprised seven blocks of semi-detached houses (14 houses in total), each linked by a single-story colonnade, with a lodge house at each end; they were redeveloped into smaller flats after suffering bomb damage during World War Two.

Morden College

Exit the Paragon into Morden Road – to the left is the entrance to the splendid Morden College, built in 1700 by John Morden as almshouses for merchants who had fallen on hard times – and turn right at the end into Blackheath

Park. Walk west towards the village, passing the majestic **St Michael & All Angels** ❹, a Gothic Revival church by architect George Smith, dating from 1830, on the corner of Pond Road. Blackheath Park is the main thoroughfare of the **Cator Estate** ❺ (see box, below), the most exclusive corner of Blackheath.

Cator Estate

The Cator Estate comprises 282 acres (114ha) to the southeast of the village. The land was purchased for £22,550 by John Cator in 1783 (which wouldn't even buy you a garage there today!) and laid out as a private estate in the 1820s. The Cator family created a development of quality houses, erecting lodge houses at the main entrances to maintain its exclusive nature. These were occupied by resident keepers engaged to ward off beggars and itinerant salesmen, and (in the early years) to distribute letters and parcels. The estate, still private, is now managed by a formidable residents' association.

At the end of Blackheath Park turn right on Lee Road, passing two striking red-brick buildings: **Blackheath Halls** ❻ – south London's finest concert hall – and the Conservatoire of Music and the Arts next door, whose alumni include Hollywood actor Gary Oldman and singer Kate Bush. Founded in 1881, it's the oldest purpose-built cultural complex in London. Go straight ahead over the roundabout to return to the centre of Blackheath Village, passing the station for the second time (if you're here on a Sunday, there's a Farmers' Market in the

station car park from 10am-2pm), and take the left-hand fork this time along Tranquil Vale.

Here, you are back in the heart of the village, where there's an abundance of cafés, restaurants and pubs. If you're ready for lunch you're spoilt for choice; favourite spots include **Hand Made Food** ❶ (number 40 – already mentioned above); **The Crown** ❼ pub (49 Tranquil Vale), a former 16-century coaching inn offering good local ales and food, a stylish interior and alfresco dining; Tziganos restaurant (17 Montpelier Vale), where passionate Italians conjure up delicious Mediterranean cuisine; and the original Zerodegrees Microbrewery (29-31 Montpelier Vale), specialising in fresh beer straight from the tanks, wood-fired pizza and pots of mussels.

After having your fill, turn right on Royal Parade and left into All Saints Drive to **All Saints, Blackheath** ❽. This imposing church was designed by Benjamin Ferrey, a pupil of Augustus Pugin

All Saints, Blackheath

Blackheath

Extending to 300 acres (121ha), Blackheath is one of the largest areas of common land in London. Its name is thought to derive from the colour of the soil, although it's also claimed the area was a burial ground for victims of the Black Death in the 14th century. The heath has been in public use since 1871 and is jointly managed by the boroughs of Lewisham and Greenwich. Despite being crossed by one of London's busiest roads (part of the A2, which follows the route of the Roman Watling Street), Blackheath is an important spot for flora and fauna. It has played host to more than its fair share of events over the centuries, including rebel gatherings, military encampments, royal meetings, religious festivals, battles, robberies by highwaymen, circuses, kite-flying tournaments and many other activities. Today, along with neighbouring Greenwich Park, it's the starting point in April for the London Marathon.

(famous for the interior of the Palace of Westminster), and dates from 1857. From here, take the northern path across **Blackheath** ❾ (see box, above), skirting Talbot Place on your left, and after 200m turn left to head up to the junction of Shooters Hill Road and Charlton Way. There's a tea hut (24-hour!)on this corner of the heath, near where the Prime Meridian line crosses the road. Shooters Hill was the haunt of highwaymen and was infamous for its gibbets (gallows) of executed felons, mentioned by Samuel Pepys in his diary in 1661. Pass Charlton Way to head north up Chesterfield Walk, which runs parallel to **Greenwich Park** ❿.

Just beyond the tennis courts, on the edge of the park, is **Queen Caroline's Bath** ⓫. This odd little plunge pool is all that remains of Montague House, which was home to Caroline of Brunswick (wife of George IV) from 1798 to 1813. Around 100m further on you come to **Ranger's House** ⓬, an elegant red-brick Georgian villa built in the Palladian style and dating from the early 1700s; since 1816 it has been the official residence of the Greenwich Park ranger. It's now managed by English Heritage and houses the magnificent Wernher Collection – jewels, paintings, porcelain, silver and more – which was amassed in the late 19th and early 20th centuries by German-born railway engineer's son, Sir Julius Wernher (1850-1912). It really does warrant a visit – see www.english-heritage.org.uk/visit/places/rangers-house-the-wernher-collection.

Greenwich Park

Go left directly opposite the house, passing a bowling green on your right, cross General Wolfe Road – named after the general whose victory over the French in Quebec in 1759 secured Canada for the British

Walk 7

– and take the footpath leading to Cade Road. Turn left then right, crossing Hyde Vale to West Grove, and cross the Grove to **Point Hill** ⑬, an exclusive corner of Greenwich which abounds in sumptuous Georgian and Regency villas. Walk down the hill, where a few steps along on the right is a viewing point with panoramic views over Greenwich, the City and East London; a panel identifies some landmark buildings.

Continue down Point Hill to Royal Hill and turn right, passing a trio of excellent pubs in quick succession: the Prince of Greenwich (a museum pub serving gourmet Italian cuisine), the Greenwich Union (global beer mecca owned by the local Meantime Brewing Company) and, next door, the **Richard I** ⑭, a traditional Young's pub with a stunning conservatory. Why not try them all?

If you can tear yourself away from your pint, continue on down Royal Hill and turn right into Gloucester Circus, keeping to the right-hand side of the central garden, and exit onto Crooms Hill, adjacent to Greenwich Park. Turn left and 100m along is the unique **Fan Museum** ⑮ (entrance fee), housed in a pair of Grade II* listed early Georgian houses (1721) that have been lovingly restored to their original character and elegance. Opened in 1991, it's the only museum in the world devoted entirely to fans and fan-making, with a collection of over 4,000 items. It also has a garden room where you can take afternoon tea on certain days (see www. thefanmuseum.org.uk).

Continue down Crooms Hill passing the **Greenwich Theatre** ⑯ on the right, which has its origins in the Rose and Crown Music Hall established over 150 years ago, and is now a vibrant theatre with a touring company. Next door is Ye Old Rose & Crown, a traditional pub serving real ales and British pub grub. Cross Nevada Street into Stockwell Street, passing the University of Greenwich and Stockwell Street Library on the right, and turn right on Greenwich

---

St Alfege Church

Dedicated to Alfege (954-1012, also spelt 'Alphege'), Archbishop of Canterbury, the church reputedly marks the spot where he was martyred by Viking raiders in 1012. The second church built here was constructed around 1290 and became the 'royal church' in Tudor times when the court was based at Greenwich. Young Henry VIII was baptised here in 1491. The current church is its third incarnation, completed in 1718; it was designed in 1714 by Nicholas Hawksmoor (1661-1736), who trained under Sir Christopher Wren and worked with him on the Royal Naval College. Notable burials include Renaissance composer Thomas Tallis (1505-1585) and General James Wolfe (1727-1759).

Food & Drink

1. **Hand Made Food**: A cosy café with mismatched furniture on Tranquil Vale – a good spot for coffee, breakfast or lunch (Tue/Sun 9am-5pm, Wed-Sat 9am-10pm, closed Mon, £).

7. **The Crown**: A former coaching inn in Blackheath Village, the Crown pub offers tasty food and ales, a bright interior and a spacious courtyard (11am-11pm, £).

14. **Richard I**: Pub on Royal Hill with a lovely garden (noon-11pm, £).

30. **Red Door**: An unusual mixture of café, gallery and shop, Red Door serves Monmouth coffee and delicious homemade cakes (10am-6pm, £).

High Road. On the opposite side is **St Alfege Church** 17 (11am-4pm, see box), an Baroque church with a long and interesting history.

Just past the church turn left down St Alfege Passage to St Alfege Park. It occupies part of the church's former churchyard, which closed for burials in 1853, and is a delightful green space with formal gardens and a children's playground. Leave the park via the northern path onto Bardsley Lane and turn right and right again at the end on Creek Road to return to Greenwich Church Street. Turn left here towards the Thames, passing the historic **Gipsy Moth** 18 pub. Up ahead is the legendary **Cutty Sark** 19, one of the world's most famous sailing ships – a record-breaking tea clipper – launched in 1869 and fully restored after a devastating fire in 2007.

To the left of the ship is a circular building, the entrance to the **Greenwich Foot Tunnel** 20 (unrestricted access) which links Greenwich with the Isle of Dogs across the Thames. It's one of London's great Victorian engineering feats (1902), with its own atmosphere and stark majesty. Turn right here to pass **Greenwich Pier** 21, where Thames ferry boats dock. From here, a Thameside path leads east, passing the magnificent **Old Royal Naval College** 22 which

Old Royal Naval College

The Queen's House

Designed by Inigo Jones, this elegant royal residence was the first consciously classical building to be constructed in Britain, and is a landmark in its architectural history. Originally part of Greenwich Palace, it was built between 1616 and 1619 for Queen Anne of Denmark (wife of James I), who died before it was completed. Now Grade I listed, the Queen's House is part of the National Maritime Museum and serves as a gallery for some of the museum's fine art collection, including contemporary art, miniatures, oil paintings, photography, prints, drawings, watercolours and sculpture.

is set back from the river on the spot where the Tudor Palace of Placentia once stood. Designed by Sir Christopher Wren, the college is now the architectural centrepiece of the Maritime Greenwich World Heritage Site, which also incorporates the Painted Hall and Chapel,

among other buildings (see www.greenwichworldheritage.org).

Just past the complex is another historic Greenwich pub, the **Trafalgar Tavern** **23**, which although named after the Battle of Trafalgar in 1805 (where Admiral Nelson died), was actually built in 1837. This graceful Regency pub is one of London's best riverside taverns, famous for its whitebait suppers, sunny terrace and glorious views.

Continue along the path to **Trinity Hospital** **24**, built in 1613 by Henry Howard, Earl of Northampton, and rebuilt in 1812 in Gothic style. An almshouse, it was founded in the last year of Howard's life and is now run by the Worshipful Company of Mercers, founded in 1394. Turn right past the hospital down Hoskins Street and right again at the end into Trafalgar Road; after some 300m it leads into Romney Road and, on the left, is the **Queen's House** **25** (see box).

Just past the Queen's House is the **National Maritime Museum** **26**, which officially opened in 1937 and is the largest museum of its kind in the world, with collections totalling over 2½ million items (see www.rmg.co.uk/national-maritime-museum for information). You could easily spend an entire day here! Next to the museum is **De Vere Devonport House** **27**, a handsome red-brick Georgian building with tall white columns, bold lines and structural symmetry, which started life in 1783 as a school building for Greenwich Hospital and is now a hotel. Turn

Painted Hall, Old Royal Naval College

Greenwich & Blackheath

Greenwich Market

Greenwich has had a market since the 14th century, although the present one dates from 1700 (and has a charter for 1,000 years!). It's actually comprised of three markets: the Antiques and Crafts Market, the Village Market and the Central Market. At the end of Turnpin Lane is the **Red Door** 30 , a café and gallery to sustain you with a hot drink and cake before you head home. From here, exit the market onto Greenwich Church Street and turn right then left into Creek Road; 50m along on the right is the Cutty Sark DLR station and the end of the walk.

left into King William Walk, where a short way along on the left (in the garden of Devonport House) is the **Throne of Earthly Kings** 28 , a modern brass sculpture by Frenchman François Hameury.

Retrace your steps to cross Romney Road and after a few metres turn left into Turnpin Lane (dating from the early 19th century) which runs along the bottom end of **Greenwich Market** 29 .

NOTE

If you're returning to central London you can travel by river – in the style of Henry VIII – on a Thames Clipper ferry (see www.thamesclippers.com).

Skyline from Greenwich Park to Canary Wharf

START & END
Hampstead

1 The Horseshoe
2 Gail's Bakery
3 Flask Walk
4 The Flask
5 Old Bathhouse
6 The Wells
7 Home of John Constable
8 Hampstead Heath

9 Goldfinger's House
10 Keats House
11 Hopkins House
12 Stanfield House
13 Perrin's Court
14 Ginger & White
15 Hampstead Antique & Craft Emporium
16 Church Row

● Places of Interest   ● Food & Drink

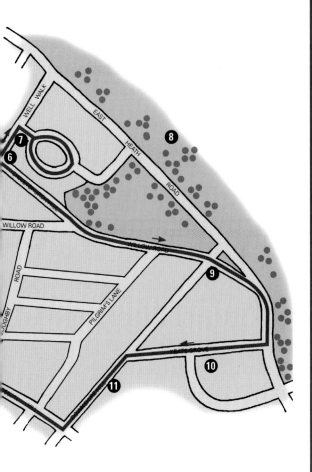

17 St John-at-Hampstead
18 Watch House
19 Judges' Walk
20 Hampstead Observatory
21 Admiral's House
22 Fenton House

23 The Holly Bush
24 Hampstead Square
25 Burgh House & Hampstead Museum
26 Buttery Café
27 Streatley Place
28 Back Lane

Hampstead

Walk 8

Distance: 3 miles (5 km)

Terrain: moderate, many hills & steps

Duration: 1½ hours

Start/End: Hampstead tube

Postcode: NW3 1QG

Hampstead is a perfectly preserved Georgian village perched on a hill 440ft (135m) above sea level in northwest London – the name comes from the Anglo-Saxon words *ham* and *stede*, which means simply 'homestead'. There has been a settlement here for over 1,000 years; early records show that King Ethelred the Unready granted Hampstead to the monastery of St Peter's at Westminster in AD 986, and it's mentioned in the *Domesday Book* of 1086. From the Middle Ages onwards, Londoners journeyed here to take the air, enjoy the fresh spring water or escape the plague raging in the city below.

Hampstead was a fashionable spa town in the 1700s, when the iron-rich waters of Hampstead Wells were a big attraction, but its popularity declined in the 18th century. The village started to expand with the opening of the railway in 1860, whereafter a wealth of luxury housing was built during the 1870s and 1880s, much of which remains today.

It was the arrival of poets such as Keats and Shelley and the artists Constable and Romney that helped establish Hampstead as a Bohemian artists' village, and it has long been famous for its intellectual, liberal, artistic, musical and literary associations. Now part of the borough of Camden, Hampstead remains a huge draw for artistic types – actors, film stars and writers – and is home to more millionaires than any other area of the UK, with some of London's most expensive housing.

Our walk follows in the footsteps of numerous illustrious figures, exploring Hampstead's most exclusive and historic neighbourhoods; visiting picturesque shopping streets, with an abundance of independent traders and boutiques, cafés, restaurants and pubs; taking in famous museums, historic churches and iconic buildings, and skirting the glorious

The Flask

heath; and strolling down the many hidden cobbled lanes, handsome squares and ancient footpaths – all of which make Hampstead such an enchanting place to roam.

Start Walking…

Ascend from Hampstead tube station (London's deepest at 192ft/58m below ground level with 320 steps if the lifts don't work!) and cross over Hampstead High Street at the lights. Go left down Heath Street and left again – just past the **Horseshoe** ❶, an elegant Victorian tavern turned gastropub – into Oriel Place. At the end is a branch of **Gail's Bakery** ❷, renowned for its excellent bread and 'baker's breakfast'.

Cross Hampstead High Street, turn left and then right down charming **Flask Walk** ❸, one of the many lanes which crisscross the village. Around 50m along this 'olde worlde' passageway on the right is **The Flask** ❹, an impressive Young's pub which gets its name from the industry which sprang from the springs of potable water that rose on Hampstead Heath. The water was

bottled and sold in the 18th century to City taverns and coffee houses for threepence a flask. Next door is La Cage Imaginaire, an elegant French-Mediterranean restaurant.

Just past Back Lane, Flask Walk widens into one of Hampstead's most picturesque and historic streets. After some 200m, the road is divided by a narrow green 'island', where on the left is the **Old Bathhouse** ❺, now luxury apartments, which has a frieze above the ground floor windows reading: 'The Wells and Camden Baths & Wash Houses 1888'. In the 19th century most workers' homes had no running water, so the public bathhouse provided both drinking water and facilities for bathing. Continue straight ahead into Well Walk, where at number 30 (just over

Flask Walk

Keats House

This Regency villa is a museum (entrance fee) and shrine dedicated to John Keats (1795-1821), one of the leading poets of the English Romantic movement. He lived here for a mere 17 months, from 1818 to 1820, before travelling to Italy where he died of tuberculosis the following year, aged just 25. Keats House contains a large variety of Keats-related material, including books, paintings and household items – along with the engagement ring he gave to his sweetheart Fanny Brawne (he died before they could marry). The romantic garden is planted to reflect its Regency heritage, and is where Keats is said to have written *Ode to a Nightingale* while sitting under a plum tree. (See www.cityoflondon.gov.uk/things-to-do/keats-house for information.)

Christchurch Hill) is **The Wells** ❻, a splendid gastropub in an elegant Georgian house. Just past the pub on the right, at number 40 (marked by a blue plaque), is the **Home of John Constable** ❼ (1776-1837), where the painter lived from 1827 until his death 10 years later. The next turning takes you into Gainsborough Gardens on the right, a circular private road of gorgeous houses, well worth a sneaky look.

Opposite the entrance to Gainsborough Gardens there's a monument marking the location of the village's Chalybeate Well (spa) in the 18th century. (Chalybeate refers to water that is high in salts containing iron, considered to be health-giving.) The inscription is dedicated to the Countess of Gainsborough and her infant son, the Earl of Gainsborough, for donating six acres of land here to be used to benefit the poor of Hampstead. The first house past Gainsborough Gardens is called Wellside and has a plaque stating that it was built in 1892 on the site of the Old Hampstead Pump Room.

Retrace your steps to The Wells and go left down Christchurch Hill to Willow Road. Here you get your first glimpse of **Hampstead Heath** ❽, one of London's largest areas of heathland extending to 790 acres (320ha). After around 200m you come to 2 Willow Road, aka **Goldfinger's House** ❾, a ground-breaking modernist home designed in 1939 by the splendidly-named, Budapest-born architect Ernő Goldfinger. It's now owned by the National Trust and open to the public (entrance fee, see www.nationaltrust.org.uk/2-willow-road for information). Continue past the house into South End Road and follow it along the heath – just opposite is Hampstead Number 1 Pond, one

John Constable

Perrin's Court

of more than 25 ponds that are scattered across the heath – then turn right into Keats Grove. **Keats House** ⑩ (see box, left) is on the left.

Continue along Keats Grove and turn left at the end into

St John-at-Hampstead

Dedicated to St John the Evangelist, this is a sumptuous Georgian church with a stunning interior. There's likely to have been a church on this site for over 1,000 years, when a charter was granted to the Benedictine monks of Westminster in 986, although the first record is from 1312. As Hampstead grew in popularity and size, the small medieval church became inadequate and run down, and was declared unusable in 1744. The present building was built in 1747, but again proved too small and was extended in 1844 by means of transepts, providing 524 extra seats. Gas lighting was installed and in 1853 the first Willis organ was built, with Henry Willis himself employed as the organist.

Downshire Hill, where some 50m on the left you pass the **Hopkins House** ⑪ (number 49b), an iconic award-winning, hi-tech home and workspace designed by architects Michael and Patty Hopkins in 1976. At the bottom of Downshire Hill, turn right along Rosslyn Hill, which becomes Pilgrim's Place and then Hampstead High Street – the heart of the village – which you crossed earlier. Just past Greenhill (a mansion block set back from the road), on the corner of Prince Arthur Road, is **Stanfield House** ⑫, which in 1855 was the grandly named 'Hampstead Public Library of General Literature and Elementary Science'. Opposite the mansion block is the entrance to Old Brewery Mews, the former site of Hampstead Brewery (1720-1921).

Hampstead High Street is lined with an abundance of eateries and foodie outlets, including the excellent Hampstead Butcher & Providore at 56 Rosslyn Hill, butcher, delicatessen, charcuterie, cheese and wine shop; the gorgeous King William IV pub and hotel at 77 High Street; Hampstead Seafoods in the

Church Row

Perhaps even more of a draw than the church is St John's hauntingly beautiful graveyard – the oldest surviving unspoiled churchyard in Greater London – whose monuments and gravestones include many of great historic significance, notably that of artist John Constable (whose

Community Market next door; and the Hampstead branch of the superb Melrose & Morgan grocer, deli and café in nearby Oriel Place.

Continue on down the high street and turn left into **Perrin's Court** ⓮ where there's a couple of favourite eateries, Villa Blanca – a cosy Italian restaurant – and **Ginger & White** ⓮, a superb café established in 2009, both offering alfresco dining. At the end turn right onto Heath Street, where just along on the right – tucked behind number 12 Heath Street – is the **Hampstead Antique & Craft Emporium** ⓯. A popular destination for collectors and antiques enthusiasts since 1967, it's packed with everything from antique and vintage furniture and collectibles, to contemporary design and craft items. Cross over and take a left into **Church Row** ⓰ – one of the village's finest streets, lined with grand 18th-century brick houses, some with white weatherboard façades – where the splendid **St John-at-Hampstead** ⓱ church (see box, page 79) is the next stop.

Food & Drink

⓶ **Gail's Bakery:** Good place for a coffee or a 'baker's breakfast' to start the day (Mon-Fri 7am-8pm, Sat-Sun 7.30am-8pm, £).

⓺ **The Wells:** A historic pub with great food; Sunday lunch (booking essential) is a particular delight (020-7794 3785, noon-11pm, £-££).

⓮ **Ginger & White:** Child-friendly café in Perrin's Court offering all-day breakfast and weekend brunch – and drinks (7.30/8.30am-5.30pm, £).

㉖ **Buttery Café:** Located in Burgh House and fully licensed, the Buttery is perfect for a drink or lunch on the garden terrace on a sunny day (Wed-Fri 10am-5pm, Sat-Sun 9.30am-5.30pm, £).

Hampstead

Hampstead Observatory

Located (since 1910) near Whitestone Pond in Hampstead at the highest point in inner London, the observatory is owned and operated by the Hampstead Scientific Society, founded in 1899. Alongside it is a weather station, which has been checked daily since 1910, providing the longest continuous record of meteorological readings in the country. The observatory offers regular free viewings of the night sky (see www.hampsteadscience.ac.uk/astro/observatory.html).

tomb is behind railings). Other worthies buried here include novelist and historian Walter Besant, writer and comedian Peter Cook, actress Kay Kendall, Labour Party leader Hugh Gaitskell, John Harrison who 'discovered' longitude and invented the marine chronometer, and various members of the distinguished du Maurier family. Singer and actress Gracie Fields lived on the other side of the churchyard at number 20 Frognal Way.

From the church go right up Holly Walk, passing a row of picturesque cottages, the diminutive St Mary Roman Catholic church (1816) on the right and Holly Berry Lane, where the **Watch House** ⓲ on the corner was Hampstead's first police station in the 1830s. At the end turn right on Mount Vernon, which has more attractive terraced houses – there's a plaque on number 7 to author Robert Louis Stevenson – and follow the road round to Frognal Rise. Head up Frognal Rise, keeping to the right, until it merges with Branch Hill (a favourite Constable location) and

after 100m, as the hill peaks, look for the steep steps on the right leading up to **Judges' Walk** ⓳ . This is an unpaved footpath on the edge of Hampstead Heath that becomes a narrow road after 100m or so. Judges' Walk is allegedly named after the justices who sought refuge here following the Great Plague of 1665 and/or the Great Fire a year later; lawyers and judges apparently transacted business here in makeshift tents until it was safe and practical to return to the City.

Admiral's House

At the end of Judges' Walk, just across Lower Terrace, is **Hampstead Observatory** ⓴ (see box, above), one of the only observatories in the world situated in the centre of a major city. Turn right here into Lower Terrace and go left where it meets Windmill Hill – almost opposite, number 2 Lower Terrace was Constable's summer home in 1821-2. Turn left again into Admiral's Walk and around halfway down on the left is **Admiral's House** ㉑ , a quirky, Grade II listed house built in the early 18th century and occupied by an eccentric former naval

Walk 8

Fenton House

lieutenant called Fountain North. He built two decks on the roof – a main deck and a quarterdeck – and mounted cannons on them, firing salutes to mark the King's birthday and notable naval victories. Sir George Gilbert Scott (1811-1878), the architect responsible for St Pancras Station and the Albert Memorial, lived here and Constable made paintings of the house a number of times. John Galsworthy (1867-1933), author of *The Forsyte Saga*, lived next door at Grove Lodge.

At the end of Admiral's Walk turn right down Hampstead Grove and some 50m along on the right is **Fenton House** ㉒ (see box, left), one of London's best small museums. It has been described by *Country Life* magazine as 'London's most enchanting country house' and its captivating garden, laid out on the side of a hill and divided into upper and lower levels, is an almost rural haven, noted for its sunken walled section, with a glasshouse, vegetable beds, a culinary herb border and flower beds. There's also a 300-year-old orchard of agreeably gnarled apple trees, producing over 30 different varieties.

Continue along Hampstead Grove past the small green into Holly Hill – the weatherboard-clad house at number 5 on the left has a blue plaque for painter George Romney, who had a studio here at the end of the 18th century – then turn left into Holly Mount and pop into **The Holly Bush** ㉓ pub. Housed in a building constructed for George Romney in the 1790s, this noted Hampstead hostelry is hidden away in a warren of passages and narrow streets. Its licence dates from 1802, although its origins apparently stretch back

---

Fenton House

A charming 17th-century merchant's house built around 1686, Fenton House (entrance fee) has remained virtually unaltered during 300 years of continuous occupation. It was purchased in 1793 by the Fentons (hence the name) who gave the house its Regency appearance. Now owned by the National Trust, the house is home to a collection of early keyboard instruments put together by the many-named Major George Henry Benton Fletcher (1866-1944). It boasts a fine collection of paintings, including some lovely portraits; artists represented in the collection include Jan Bruegel, Albrecht Dürer, John Russell, Francis Sartorius and G. F. Watts. There's also a world-class collection of English, European and Oriental porcelain, plus 17th-century needlework pictures and Georgian furniture.

to 1643 – diarist James Boswell and polymath Samuel Johnson are reputed to have been patrons, while more recent regulars included John Constable and scientist Michael Faraday. Leave the pub and carry on down Holly Mount – which offers wonderful views over the city's skyline – and descend the steep Holly Mount Steps to Heath Street.

Turn left and, after passing the shops and restaurants, turn right past the Friends Meeting House into leafy **Hampstead Square 24**, lined with grand 18th-century houses with walled gardens. Follow the 'square' as it loops round to the right into Elm Row, and take the narrow cobbled passage – down some step steps

on the left (just past number 10) – leading to New End and the popular Hampstead Lounge & Jazz Club. Turn left to New End, passing the former Hampstead Union Workhouse opened in 1800, which later became a hospital (closed in 1986) and is now an apartment block. The road leads into New End Square (which isn't a square either!) straight ahead, where some 50m along on the left is **Burgh House & Hampstead Museum 25** (see box, left), which is also home to the lovely **Buttery Café 26** and its pretty garden, full of nooks and crannies, a civilised place to enjoy lunch or a glass of wine.

Retrace your steps a few metres and take New End (the eastern end of the road) on the left and continue past Boades Mews into **Streatley Place 27** and follow it around to the left, where it becomes a steep alleyway, passing New End Primary School. At the end of the alley go up the steps to cobbled **Back Lane 28**, with its pretty colourful cottages, and turn right then left on Heath Street. Walk down to the junction with Hampstead High Street to reach Hampstead tube station and the end of the walk.

Burgh House

A Queen Anne-style house built in 1704, Burgh House (noon-5pm, Wed-Fri & Sun, closed Mon-Tue & Sat) is one of the oldest houses in Hampstead, with original panelled rooms and staircase. This handsome building is named after the Reverend Allatson Burgh, who purchased it in 1822. Among its many tenants was Rudyard Kipling's daughter, Elsie Bambridge, in the '30s. Nowadays, the Grade I listed house is home to Hampstead Museum, which traces Hampstead's history from prehistoric times to the present day, and holds over 3,000 objects (see www.burghhouse.org.uk).

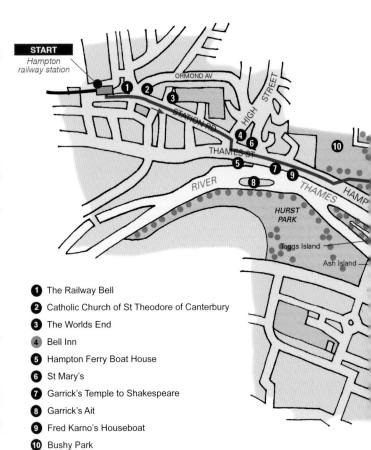

1. The Railway Bell
2. Catholic Church of St Theodore of Canterbury
3. The Worlds End
4. Bell Inn
5. Hampton Ferry Boat House
6. St Mary's
7. Garrick's Temple to Shakespeare
8. Garrick's Ait
9. Fred Karno's Houseboat
10. Bushy Park
11. Waterhouse Woodland Garden
12. Diana Fountain
13. Hampton Court Palace
14. Hampton Court Maze
15. Tiltyard Café
16. Old Court House
17. Mute Swan
18. Mitre
19. Hampton Court Bridge
20. Henry's Kitchen

Places of Interest   Food & Drink

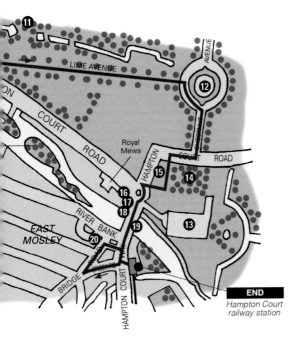

END
*Hampton Court
railway station*

Hampton

Distance: 2½ miles (4 km)
Terrain: easy, some moderate hills
Duration: 1½ hours
Start: Hampton rail
End: Hampton Court rail
Postcode: TW12 2HU

HAMPTON

amous for its royal connections, including a picture-perfect palace and a magnificent royal park, Hampton is just 13mi (21km) southwest of central London and full of semi-rural charm. Hampton sits on the north side of the River Thames, and its name is thought to come from the Anglo-Saxon words *hamm* – a large bend in a river – and *ton*, meaning a farmstead or settlement. It was originally located in the county of Middlesex, which was abolished in 1965, and is now administered by the London borough of Richmond-upon-Thames.

The area has been settled for over 4,000 years, although the village of Hampton grew up in the Middle Ages around the parish church of St Mary's. Modern Hampton has evolved to include three villages – Hampton, Hampton Wick to the east and Hampton Hill to the north – collectively known as the Hamptons. At their heart are Bushy Park, London's second-largest royal park after Richmond, and Hampton Court Palace, Britain's finest surviving Tudor building.

The Hamptons are highly sought after due to their proximity to the river and parks, and to the towns of Richmond and Kingston, their good schools and 'reasonable' property prices, which, while not cheap (this is London after all!), are more affordable than in some neighbouring areas.

Our walk commences in Hampton and meanders along the Thames, taking in a ferry and a folly, before exploring part of Bushy Park and Hampton Court Palace, finishing up in Hampton Court village on the south bank of the river.

Start Walking…

From Hampton railway station turn left along Station Road, passing **The Railway Bell** ❶ on the left, a traditional village pub with a large patio – and the first of many delightful inns along the walk. Diagonally across from the pub is Hampton Village Green, a popular venue for games, picnics and community events, while further along Station Road on the left is the **Catholic Church of St Theodore of Canterbury** ❷. Theodore of Tarsus (602-690) was Archbishop of Canterbury from 668 to 690, and is best known for his reforms of the English church and the establishment of a school in Canterbury.

Carry on along Station Road, passing **The Worlds End** ❸, a handsome Victorian pub with a large garden, on the left, and some fine Georgian townhouses and pretty cottages on the right. At the end of Station Road turn right on the High Street and left along Thames Street opposite the river. Here, you can take a pit stop at the **Bell Inn** ❹; built in 1892 (replacing an older hotel that burnt down), it's an award-winning gastropub with a large garden overlooking the Thames.

Opposite the pub, the **Hampton Ferry Boat House** ❺ operates the oldest ferry on the Thames. From April to October, it transports foot passengers (plus bicycles and pushchairs) to Hurst Park in Molesey on the south bank. Records show the ferry service

> ### St Mary's
>
> St Mary's church stands at the heart of the village and has done so for over 650 years. Records show that the original church was founded here in 1342 by monks from the Essex Priory of Takeley, but it's likely there was a place of worship on this site even earlier. The present church dates from 1831 when the previous building was no longer large enough for the growing congregation. Worship took place in the Great Hall of Hampton Court Palace while the church was being rebuilt.

has been in operation since 1514, although it's said to be much older; certainly, boats and barges have moored to load and unload goods here for 1,000 years. Next door to the Bell Inn is the parish church of **St Mary's** ❻ (see box), one of the most historic and prominent landmarks in Hampton village.

A short way past the church on the riverside is a striking little octagonal folly set amidst lush lawns. This is **Garrick's Temple to Shakespeare** ❼ (Sun 2-5pm, April to October), built in 1756, while the garden is known as Garrick's Lawn. The renowned

Hampton Ferry Boat House & St Mary's

Walk 9

Ait or Eyot

The word ait (or eyot) comes from the Old English for a small island in a river or lake – usually long and narrow in shape – and refers particularly to islands in the Thames and its tributaries. There are a number of aits/eyots along this stretch of the river, including Tagg's Island (accessed via a road bridge) and neighbouring tree-covered Ash Island, both a few hundred metres upstream.

---

actor-manager David Garrick (1717-1779) – who lived in Hampton – built the temple to celebrate the genius of William Shakespeare (1564-1616), in whose plays he often acted; it houses a life-size statue of his hero by the sculptor Roubiliac. It's now a museum, concert venue and mini theatre, and a memorial to the life and career of Garrick – and, reputedly, the world's only shrine to the Bard. Opposite the garden is **Garrick's Ait** ❽ (or eyot – see box, above), one of many residential islands on this stretch of the Thames.

Fred Karno's Houseboat

Another unique Hampton icon, **Fred Karno's Houseboat** ❾, is moored here. Called *Astoria*, it was constructed in 1911 for impresario Fred Karno who numbered Charlie Chaplin among his clients. Karno, who owned Tagg's Island and built its landmark Karsino Hotel resort, was determined to have the best houseboat on the river, and he designed the *Astoria* so that it could accommodate a 90-piece orchestra playing on deck! The houseboat is now owned by Pink Floyd guitarist David Gilmour, who converted it into a recording studio in the '80s.

Diana Fountain

A little further along on the left is **Bushy Park** ❿ (see box, right) which is open 24 hours to pedestrians (except during the annual deer cull). Enter via Hampton Gate and follow the path along Lime Avenue, with the glorious **Waterhouse Woodland Garden** ⓫ on your left. Continue along the avenue for around half a mile (1km) to the **Diana Fountain** ⓬ in the centre of a round pond. The striking fountain features a gilded bronze statue of the goddess Diana on a fountain, surrounded by bronzes of four boys, four water nymphs and four shells. It was designed by Hubert Le Sueur in 1637 at the request of King Charles I (for his wife Henrietta Maria).

Bushy Park

The second-largest of London's royal parks after Richmond Park, Bushy Park covers an area of 1,100 acres (445ha) and, like Richmond, is a traditional deer park. The name Bushy Park was first recorded in 1604, although its origins date from 1491 when Giles d'Aubrey (Lord Chamberlain to Henry VII) enclosed 400 acres (162ha) of farmland. When Henry VIII appropriated Hampton Court Palace from Cardinal Wolsey in 1529, he also assumed ownership of the three parks that surrounded it: Hare Warren, Middle Park and Bushy Park, which comprise today's park. Henry created a deer chase and built a brick wall around the park, a section of which remains. Today, the park strikes a balance between wilderness and formality, its rough grassland and plantations complemented by formal avenues of lime and chestnut trees. (For more information, see www.royalparks.org. uk/parks/bushy-park.)

From the fountain take Chestnut Avenue south to cross Hampton Court Road and enter the grounds of **Hampton Court Palace** ❸ (see box, page 91). Grade I listed, Hampton Court is one of two surviving royal palaces to be previously occupied by Henry VIII (the other is St James's in central London). It's maintained by an independent charity, Historic Royal Palaces, and is a major tourist attraction. The palace is set in Hampton Court Park (also called Home Park), which extends to 750 acres (304ha), including 60 acres (26ha) of formal palace gardens set within a loop of the Thames. The park isn't of particular interest, the star being the palace's spectacular gardens, with a feast of formal period features, sparkling fountains and glorious displays of over 200,000 flowering bulbs.

The downside of visiting the palace and its gardens (not accessible separately) is the considerable entrance fee: £25 adults, £20 concessions, £12.50 children from March 2018 (cheaper if you book online). Bear in mind that if you decide to stump up the entrance fee, you should allow **at least** three hours to see the main palace rooms, and can easily spend a whole day exploring the palace and gardens. (See www.hrp.org.uk/hampton-court-palace for information.)

Just past Hampton Court Gate, is **Hampton Court Maze** ❹. Designed by George London and Henry Wise and commissioned around 1700 by William III, it's the most famous maze in the world, covering a third of an acre. You can visit the maze (entrance fee) separately from the palace and gardens. Admission to the formal gardens on the East and South Fronts is free for just one hour (9-10am) each morning and on nine days during the year, including during the RHS Hampton Court Palace Flower Show in July (see www.rhs.org.uk/shows-events/rhs-hampton-court-palace-flower-show).

Food & Drink

(4) Bell Inn: Award-winning gastropub in Hampton village with superb river views (11am-midnight, £).

(17) Mute Swan: Historic pub opposite Hampton Court Palace offering good food and ales (11am-11pm, £).

(20) Henry's Kitchen: Eco-friendly restaurant in Hampton Court village serving traditional British and Mediterranean dishes (8am-6pm, Wed 8.30pm, Thu-Sat 10pm, £).

From the maze, go right and walk along the western perimeter of the Wilderness, where you pass the **Tiltyard Café (15)** (mixed reviews). The Wilderness – as used here, the term refers to a place to wander, rather than an uncultivated area – is an English version of a French *bosquet* or small plantation, and would have comprised 18ft (5.5m) high hornbeam hedges, with interstices planted with elm.

Continue past the Rose Garden, turn right and exit via the main entrance through a pair of splendid gates onto Hampton Court Way and cross over the road. To the left (opposite the palace) in Hampton Court Road is the **Old Court House (16)**, once the home of Sir Christopher Wren (1632-1723) – look for the blue plaque. When Wren was appointed Royal Surveyor by Charles II in 1669, he was given free lodgings at each of the royal palaces, including Hampton Court. He relinquished his role as Royal Surveyor in 1718 (at the age of 86!) and should have vacated the property then, but Queen Anne granted him a 50-year lease in lieu of overdue payments for his work on St Paul's Cathedral.

Return to Hampton Court Way opposite the palace gates, where there are two excellent establishments for a late lunch: the **Mute Swan (17)** and the **Mitre (18)** next door. The Mute Swan is a wonderful characterful pub with a spacious bar, upstairs restaurant and courtyard, while the Mitre has an idyllic riverside restaurant. Continue past the Mitre and cross **Hampton Court Bridge (19)**, the fourth bridge on the site, designed by Sir Edward Lutyens and engineer W. P. Robinson and opened in 1933. On the south

Old Court House

Hampton

Hampton Court Palace

Hampton Court Palace (Grade I listed, entrance fee) is a vast royal palace covering 6 acres (2.5ha) situated on the Thames. It was built in 1514 for Cardinal Thomas Wolsey – Lord Chancellor and favourite of Henry VIII – and was seized by the King in 1529 when Wolsey fell from favour. Henry made it his main London residence and greatly enlarged it. William III made extensive changes in the following century (he intended Hampton Court to rival Versailles) but he lost interest in 1694 after the death of his wife Queen Mary, leaving the palace in two distinct contrasting architectural styles: domestic Tudor and Baroque. The last British monarch to live at Hampton Court was George II who died in 1760. It was opened to the public in 1838.

Carry on down Hampton Court Way and just before the railway station cross over to Creek Road. Follow the road round to the right and at the roundabout go right into Bridge Road, where there's a variety of shops (including antiques shops) and a good choice of cafés, pubs and restaurants. One of our favourites is **Henry's Kitchen** 20 at number 9. From here, follow Bridge Road round to the right and cross Hampton Court Way again to reach Hampton Court railway station and the end of the walk.

bank of the Thames is Hampton Court village – actually located in East Molesey, Surrey – an attractive spot with a wide choice of shops and eateries.

Hampton Court Palace

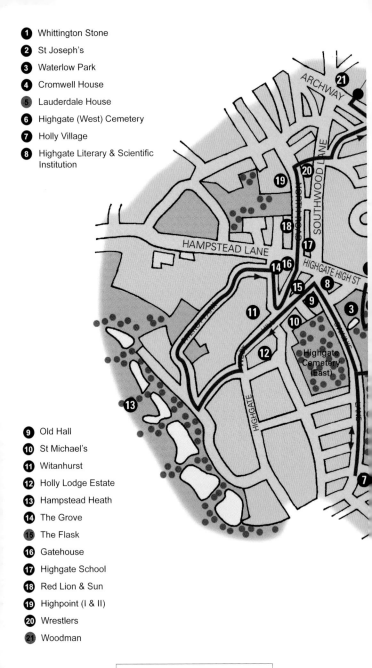

1. Whittington Stone
2. St Joseph's
3. Waterlow Park
4. Cromwell House
5. Lauderdale House
6. Highgate (West) Cemetery
7. Holly Village
8. Highgate Literary & Scientific Institution

9. Old Hall
10. St Michael's
11. Witanhurst
12. Holly Lodge Estate
13. Hampstead Heath
14. The Grove
15. The Flask
16. Gatehouse
17. Highgate School
18. Red Lion & Sun
19. Highpoint (I & II)
20. Wrestlers
21. Woodman

● Places of Interest ● Food & Drink

END
Highgate

SHEPHERDS HILL

ROAD

START
Archway

HIGHGATE

DARTMOUTH

HILL

PARK

HILL

WALK 10

Highgate

Walk 10

Distance: 3 miles (5 km)
Terrain: moderate, some steep hills
Duration: 1½ hours
Start: Archway tube
End: Highgate tube
Postcode: N19 5RQ

eeply desirable Highgate village, with its glorious Georgian houses and generous green spaces – including one of London's most splendid cemeteries – is located in the north of the city, spread across the boroughs of Camden, Haringey and Islington. A close neighbour of Hampstead, Highgate abuts the eastern part of Hampstead Heath, and has some of the best views in London, being 423ft (129m) above sea level at its highest point.

Highgate has its roots in the 14th century, when it was part of the Bishop of London's hunting estate; the name was first recorded in 1354 when the bishop erected a tollgate, which is marked today by the Gatehouse pub. Highgate grew up around today's Pond Green, where villagers once drew their water. From the 16th century it became a popular country retreat for wealthy city dwellers, and its allure accelerated during the 17th and 18th centuries, when grand mansions were built along Highgate Hill.

Until late Victorian times, Highgate was a distinct village outside London, sitting astride the Great North Road. The railway arrived in 1867, but Highgate largely escaped the tide of suburbia that overwhelmed other villages. Today, it's home to a wealth of beautiful 17th and 18th-century architecture and still has the feel of a village, with its leafy streets, abundance of historic pubs, quaint shops and grand Victorian cemetery.

Our walk takes us up Highgate Hill to Waterlow Park, skirts Highgate Cemetery and goes along South Grove to Merton Lane, then along the edge of Hampstead Heath back to the Grove and its fine old houses. It continues up the Old North Road past Highgate School and some fine historic pubs, before terminating at Highgate tube station.

Start Walking…

From Archway tube station, take the Highgate exit and walk up Highgate Hill, a section of the historic Great North Road. This was once part of the mail coach highway between London and Scotland and the stretch between Archway and Highgate tube stations was served by Europe's first cable-car tramway from 1884 to 1909. Around 100m up on the left is the **Whittington Stone** ❶, a monumental stone surmounted with a sculpted cat, enclosed by railings. Legend has it the stone marks the spot where Dick Whittington (ca. 1354-1423), a

celebrated four-times Lord Mayor of London, heard the Bow bells ring out urging him to 'turn again' and change his mind about leaving London. Continuing the theme, just past the stone is the huge Whittington Hospital and a few hundred metres further on is the Whittington Stone pub.

Lauderdale House

Waterlow Park

Originally the grounds of Lauderdale House, this 29-acre (11.7ha) park takes its name from the house's last owner, Sir Sidney Waterlow (1822-1906). It was built in 1582 for Sir Richard Martin (d 1617), the Master of the Mint and thrice Lord Mayor of London, and has a rich and interesting history. The Earl of Lauderdale owned it for a while (hence the name) and it's said Nell Gwynne was (briefly) resident. In 1889, Sir Sidney gave the house and grounds to London County Council 'for the enjoyment of Londoners' and as 'a garden for the gardenless'. The house is now an arts and education centre, while the tranquil park – which offers some of the best cityscape views in London – has formal terraced gardens, three ponds fed by natural springs, tree-lined walkways, herbaceous borders and verdant expanses of lawn.

Continue up the hill, where just before the junction with Dartmouth Park Hill, is **St Joseph's Roman Catholic Church** ❷, its tower topped by a copper dome weighing some 2,000 tons. The church has a splendid Italianate interior with a vaulted ceiling painted by Nathaniel Westlake in 1891 (one of his finest works) and an outstanding organ by William Hill and Sons. Just past the church is **Waterlow Park** ❸ (see box, left), and opposite the park, at number 104 Highgate Hill, is **Cromwell House** ❹, now the home of the Ghana High Commission; dating from 1638, it's a magnificent example of the many fine 17th-century red-brick

Highgate Cemetery

Now Grade I listed, Highgate Cemetery was one of London's 'Magnificent Seven' cemeteries, intended to take the strain from the city's overcrowded churchyards. Designed by Stephen Geary and landscaped by David Ramsey, it opened in 1839 and was soon the capital's most fashionable cemetery, thanks to its stunning architecture and elevation. The cemetery (entrance fee) covers 37 acres (15ha) and is divided into two parts – the original West Cemetery and the East Cemetery, which opened in 1856. The West Cemetery is accessible only by guided tour but the East Cemetery – where Karl Marx ('workers of all lands unite') is buried – can be visited independently.

houses that line the streets of Highgate.

Highgate Hill leads up to Highgate High Street, with its abundance of independent shops, cafés, pubs and restaurants (should you want a quick detour), but for now cross the road and enter Waterlow Park; **Lauderdale House** ⑤ , just ahead, has a pleasant café (8.30am-5pm). Leave the house via the terrace gardens, go right on the main path between the two ponds and exit onto Swain's Lane. Almost opposite is the entrance to **Highgate (West) Cemetery** ⑥ (see box, left), one of London's most famous burial grounds.

Turn left to take a short detour along the boundary of the East Cemetery and some 500m further on, on the corner of Chester Road, is **Holly Village** ⑦ . Built in 1865, this fairy-tale confection of 12 houses, complete with turrets, spires and gables, was designed in an elaborate Gothic style by Henry Astley Darbishire for Baroness Angela Burdett-Coutts, and is London's first example of a gated development.

Retrace your steps up Swain's Lane and make the steep climb to the village. On the right at the end of Swain's Lane in South Grove is the **Highgate Literary and Scientific Institution** ⑧ , which hosts a lively programme of lectures, films, courses and exhibitions. Founded in 1839 by Harry Chester, this thriving organisation is the only community institution of its kind in London. Opposite is Pond Square, the site of the original village green and pond from where villagers drew water until piped water arrived in the mid-19th century.

Holly Village

From Swain's Lane turn left along South Grove to see the **Old Hall** ❾ on the left, the remains of Arundel House, built in the early 16th century by one of Elizabeth I's courtiers. From 1610 it was the home of Thomas Howard, Earl of Arundel, who entertained many distinguished guests here, including philosopher and scientist Francis Bacon, who died here in 1626. Just past the hall is **St Michael's** ❿ , the parish church of Highgate village, with the highest elevation of any church in London. Consecrated in 1832, it was designed by Lewis Vulliamy, a pioneer of neo-Gothic style, and built by William and Lewis Cubitt.

Holly Lodge Estate

The Grove

This collection of exquisite semi-detached houses occupies what was once the site of two estates – Arundel House (now Old Hall, see left) and Dorchester House. The houses were built by city merchant William Blake around 1688 and have had some famous residents. Poet and writer Samuel Taylor Coleridge (1772-1834) – author of *The Rime of the Ancient Mariner* – lived with the Gillman family at number 3 from 1823 until his death in 1834, while the author J. B. Priestley later lived in the same house (there are blue plaques to both Coleridge and Priestley). More recently, number 5 was home to George Michael; an informal memorial garden to the singer was created opposite after his death in 2016.

Bear left onto Highgate West Hill and on the right is the gatehouse to **Witanhurst** ⓫ , a vast Georgian Revival mansion, built 1913-20 by Sir Arthur Crosfield and reputedly the second-largest house in London after Buckingham Palace. Now Grade II* listed and worth over £300m, it's owned by a Russian billionaire. Around 200m further on, on the left, is the private gated **Holly Lodge Estate** ⓬ . Built in the '20s, it includes pioneering mansion blocks up to five stories high – designed to house single women who'd moved to London to work as secretaries and clerks – united by timber details, gable roofs with finials, red tiles, casement windows and balconies, and offering spectacular views of the London skyline.

Cross Highgate West Hill, turn right and go left down Merton Lane – bordered by large properties screened by towering trees – which terminates at the eastern border of **Hampstead Heath** ⓭ , where you turn right onto Millfield Lane. If you follow the lane north along the edge of the heath it takes you past some of the Hampstead Ponds and to Kenwood House. The route continues along Fitzroy Park on the right – there's a sign saying private road – which you follow round to the right past the Fitzroy Park Allotments (for which there's a 40-year waiting list!). This exclusive enclave is named after Charles Fitzroy, the first Lord Southampton, who built a mansion here in the 18th century. It loops around the back of the Witanhurst mansion (see above) and finally meets **The Grove** ⑭ (see box, page 97), where you turn right.

The Flask

At the end of The Grove turn left on Highgate West Hill, and look for **The Flask** ⑮ pub just up on the right. Named after the containers of spring water once collected on Hampstead Heath, it's an 18th-century coaching inn with wooden beams, an original shutter-window bar, bottle glass windows, and a plethora of nooks and crannies. There are even a couple of ghosts: a Spanish barmaid who hanged herself and a uniformed Cavalier. Carry on up the hill, passing a grass-covered reservoir on the left, constructed by the New River Company in 1854

when Highgate got its first piped water supply. At the end (on the left) is the **Gatehouse** ⑯, a rare combination of pub and award-winning fringe theatre, Upstairs at the Gatehouse, producing a varied programme of drama, musicals and fringe theatre productions. This is thought to have been the site of an inn since the 14th century, although the mock Tudor façade only dates from 1905.

Opposite the pub is an ornate red-brick chapel (Highgate Old Chapel) belonging to **Highgate School** ⑰, with the main school buildings behind it. It's one of London's oldest public (independent) schools, founded in 1565 by Sir Roger Cholmeley as a free grammar school. From here you make a short detour to the right along Highgate High Street to Southwood Lane, where behind the school at numbers 15-37 are the Wollaston and Pauncefoot Almshouses, consisting of six on-bedroom cottages. They were founded by Sir John Wollaston in the 17th century and rebuilt by Sir Edward Pauncefoot in 1722. Almost opposite the almshouses at 22 Southwood Lane is Avalon, the childhood home of author-explorer Mary Kingsley (1862-1900), marked by a blue plaque.

Return to the Gatehouse and continue up the North Road, where there are many fine 17th and 18th-century houses. Poet John Betjeman lived at number 12 and A. E. Housman (1859-1936) – author of *A Shropshire Lad* – at number 17 from 1886-1905. On the left is the handsome **Red Lion & Sun** ⑱, yet

Highpoint

another of Highgate's superb historic pubs, with a reputation for outstanding food. Some 250m further along, number 92 on the right has a plaque to Charles Dickens who lived here briefly in 1832. Opposite are **Highpoint (I & II)** **⑲** apartment blocks – fine examples of early International Style architecture, designed by Russian Berthold Lubetkin in 1933-8. Turn right into Park Walk, a pedestrian walkway running alongside the

Wrestlers ⑳ , another glorious hostelry with a history stretching back to 1547.

At the end of the path cross Southwood Lane into Jackson's Lane, named after a 19-century fox-hunting colonel who lived in the house with striking bay windows, immediately on the left. The lane was once a footpath across Highgate Common, and has some lovely 18th-century mansions. At the end turn left into Archway Road, where Highgate tube station is around 100m up on the right. If you fancy a drink or a meal, the **Woodman ㉑** gastropub is a few steps further along.

Food & Drink

⑥ Lauderdale House Café: Tranquil licensed café in Waterlow Park with an attractive terrace (8.30am-4pm, Sat/Sun 9.30am-6pm £).

⑮ The Flask: Popular 18th-century pub in Highgate village with a large garden, good ales – and ghosts (11.30am-11pm, £).

㉑ Woodman: Close to Highgate tube station, serving delicious seasonal British cuisine (9am-midnight, £).

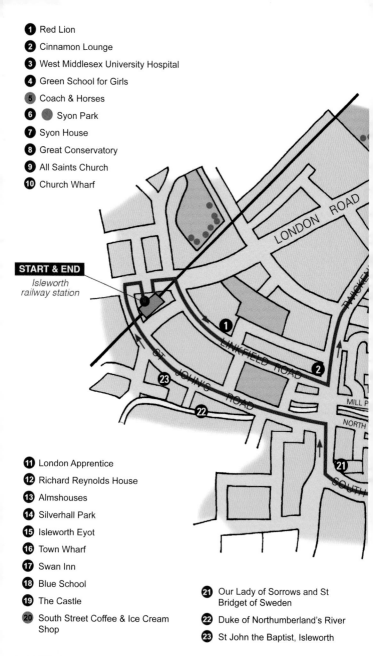

1 Red Lion
2 Cinnamon Lounge
3 West Middlesex University Hospital
4 Green School for Girls
5 Coach & Horses
6 ● Syon Park
7 Syon House
8 Great Conservatory
9 All Saints Church
10 Church Wharf

START & END
Isleworth railway station

11 London Apprentice
12 Richard Reynolds House
13 Almshouses
14 Silverhall Park
15 Isleworth Eyot
16 Town Wharf
17 Swan Inn
18 Blue School
19 The Castle
20 South Street Coffee & Ice Cream Shop

21 Our Lady of Sorrows and St Bridget of Sweden
22 Duke of Northumberland's River
23 St John the Baptist, Isleworth

● Places of Interest ● Food & Drink

LONDON ROAD
LINKFIELD ROAD
ST JOHN'S ROAD
MILL P
NORTH
SOUTH

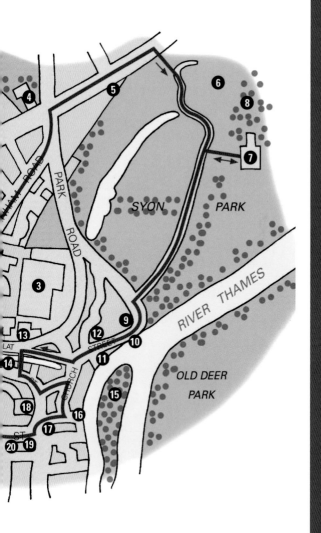

Isleworth

Distance: 4 miles (6½ km)

Terrain: easy

Duration: 2 hours

Start/End: Isleworth rail

Postcode: TW7 4BY

ISLEWORTH

Isleworth (pronounced Izle-worth) is a suburb in west London tucked between Brentford and Hounslow. At its heart is 'Old Isleworth', a London 'village' nestling along a picturesque stretch of the Thames, with an interesting history, splendid architecture – including some fine terraced houses from the 18th and early 19th centuries – and close proximity to handsome Syon House and its glorious park.

There's evidence of a settlement here dating back over 4,000 years; Neolithic remains have been found between Syon House and Brentford. The earliest recorded mention of Isleworth is an Anglo-Saxon charter of 677 when it was called Gīslheresuuyrth (an 'enclosure belonging to a man called Gīslhere'), and by the time of the *Domesday Book* (1086) it was a sizeable village. By the 13th century Isleworth was part of a manorial estate owned by Richard, 1st Earl of Cornwall (brother of Henry III), which Henry V gifted to Syon Abbey in 1422. Following the dissolution of the monasteries (1536-41), much land fell into private ownership and Isleworth began to develop into a wealthy residential area. In 1594, the manor was granted to Henry Percy (9th Earl of Northumberland) by Queen Elizabeth I and Syon House has remained in the Percy family ever since.

Isleworth's riverside was a commercial hub in the Middle Ages and by the 18th century it was well known for its river-based industries, orchards and market gardens. A century later – with the coming of the railways in 1849 – it had become more industrialised, with manufactured goods joining the traditional flour mills and breweries. Pears soap was made in Isleworth for a hundred years from 1862.

Although new developments in recent decades are changing the face of Old Isleworth, it remains something of a 'hidden' backwater, with picturesque views and an abundance of character, and our walk takes us through its most interesting streets, across Syon Park and along a lovely stretch of the Thames.

Start Walking…

Leave Isleworth railway station and turn right on London Road and right again on Linkfield Road, passing the **Red Lion** ❶ on the left, an award-winning pub with live music, and St John's Gardens on the right. Go left at the end onto Twickenham Road, passing the **Cinnamon Lounge** ❷ Indian restaurant. A short way down on the right is the **West Middlesex University Hospital** ❸, a renowned teaching hospital opened in 1894. Around 400m past the hospital you return to London Road. Opposite the junction, to the left of Spur Road,

---

Syon House

Syon House and Park (both Grade I listed) comprise one of England's finest estates. The name derives from Syon Abbey (named after Mount Zion in the Holy Land), a medieval monastery of the Bridgettine Order, which was founded nearby in 1415 on land granted by Henry V, but dissolved in 1539 by Henry VIII. It's been the home of the Percy family (the Dukes of Northumberland) since 1594. In 1761, architect and interior designer Robert Adam (1728-1792) and landscape designer Lancelot 'Capability' Brown (1716-1783) were commissioned to redesign the house and estate. In the event, only five rooms – including the Great Hall, State Dining Room and Long Gallery – were completed in the Neo-classical style. Nevertheless, Syon House is feted as Adam's early English masterpiece and is the finest surviving example of his revolutionary use of colour. The house also contains a sumptuous collection of period furniture and paintings. (See www.syonpark.co.uk for information.)

Syon House (all)

is the highly-rated **Green School for Girls** ❹ – the name comes from its original green uniform – a secondary school and sixth form with academy status. The school started life as a Sunday school in 1796 and educated girls who'd been rejected by the heavily oversubscribed Blue School (see page 106).

Great Conservatory

Go right along London Road, where soon after passing the **Coach & Horses** ❺ – a bright and welcoming open-plan pub with a conservatory and terrace – you reach the main entrance gate to **Syon Park** ❻. The Lion Gate, as it's sometimes called, was designed (it's said) by Robert Adam and is surmounted by a lion, emblem of the Percy family. Unfortunately this impressive gate is kept locked and instead you must enter the park further along via the pedestrian entrance (or Duchess Gate) opposite Rowan Road. A footpath leads across the park to Park Road, where you turn right to bypass the car park, behind which is the visitor centre, garden centre and, to the right, **Syon House** ❼ (entrance fee, open March-Oct, see box, page 103).

One of London's (and the UK's) best historic stately homes, the house is well worth a visit if you have a couple of hours to spare. It remains the London home of the Duke of Northumberland and is the

> ### Church Wharf
>
> In the days of Henry VIII, Church Wharf was known as Isleworth Stairs, and was the docking place for the ferry connecting the village and Syon House to Richmond Palace on the south bank of the Thames. In 1541, Queen Catherine Howard boarded the Royal Barge from Isleworth Stairs – after three months' incarceration at Syon House – for her fateful journey to the Tower of London. A decade later, another tragic young girl, Lady Jane Grey, made the same journey (in 1553) to accept the throne as Queen of England, only to be imprisoned after nine days as monarch and later executed. Today, Church Wharf is a free draw dock, meaning that boats can moor without paying fees.

last surviving ducal residence in Greater London to retain its country estate. Syon Park covers 200 acres (80ha), including 40 acres (16ha) of gardens, an ornamental lake, and an extensive collection of rare trees and plants. One of the crowning glories of the gardens is the **Great Conservatory** ❽ (behind the visitor centre), designed by Charles Fowler and completed in 1830; it was the first large-scale conservatory to be built out of metal and glass. If you want to see the formal gardens and conservatory you must buy a

All Saints Church

Isleworth riverfront

ticket, or you can combine it with a visit to the house. If you just fancy a drink or lunch, there's the Garden Kitchen located in the Wyevale Garden Centre.

From the house, continue south along Park Road, passing the Garden Room (and events venue) on the left, and exit the park via the gate in the southwest corner, turning left onto Church Street. Follow the road round to **All Saints Church** ⑨ which faces the River Thames. This is the oldest parish church in Isleworth, although the only parts to survive the ravages of time are the 15th-century stone tower and the foundations. Just in front of the church is **Church Wharf** ⑩ (see box, left), while just off to the left, on the edge of Syon Park and almost out of sight, is the resplendent Old Isleworth Boating Pavilion (in pink, green and white), built in the 1770s by the influential architect James Wyatt. At low tide you can step down onto the river bank for a better look.

At the end of Church Wharf is the **London Apprentice** ⑪ , a Grade II* listed pub, dating from the early 18th century and first recorded as a licensed inn in 1731. The name harks back to the time when apprentices of the

City Livery Companies used to row up the Thames on their days off (and stop for a beer!). You're now in the heart of what's known as 'Old Isleworth'. Church Street contains most of the village's oldest houses, including **Richard Reynolds House** ⑫ (just past the London Apprentice on the right), which commemorates a monk of Syon Abbey who was executed in 1535 for refusing to renounce his Catholic faith.

Continue along Church Street and turn right on Mill Plat ('plat' is merely a plot of ground), the site of the former Isleworth Flour Mill. The Plat is where Sir Thomas Ingram, Chancellor of the Duchy of Lancaster, founded **Ingram's Almshouses** ⑬ in 1664 – they comprise six bed-sitter terraced bungalows, which you pass on the right after around 100m. Soon after (where the path widens) take the path to the left over the Duke of Northumberland's River (see below) through enchanting **Silverhall Park** ⑭ to North Street. Turn left here and left again into Manor House Way at the roundabout; this marks the site of Richard Earl of Cornwall's medieval manor house, though modern buildings dominate

London Apprentice

now and no trace of the manor remains.

At the end of the road you're back on Church Street. Opposite is **Isleworth Eyot** 15 , a teardrop-shaped eyot (or ait – an island in a river) that extends to 8.6 acres (3.5ha). It was once a centre of production for osier, a willow used to weave baskets to carry fruit and vegetables at markets. It's now a bird sanctuary, run by the London Wildlife Trust and home to some 60 species.

Church Street continues south into Lower Square, which meets Swan Street, where there are two interesting pubs. Turn left towards the river for the **Town Wharf** 16 , a Sam Smith's pub resembling a Swiss chalet. It's off the beaten track and serves a good-value pint with a view of Isleworth Ait. Alternatively, turn right for the **Swan Inn** 17 near the junction with North Street; it's a traditional Victorian pub with a garden, serving excellent cask ales and

good pub grub. Nearby Swan Court, White Lion Court and Swan Street have been regenerated to provide new homes and better access to the riverside. Off to the right at the end of Swan Street is North Street, the site of the **Blue School** 18 (see box, below).

From the Swan Inn, turn left on Upper Square and right on South Street. Opposite is **The Castle** 19 pub, a traditional Young's 'sports' pub, dating from the late 18th century, with a separate restaurant. On the next block is the **South Street Coffee & Ice Cream Shop** 20 , perfect for a coffee or a cornet.

Old Blue School

The Blue School

The current Blue School in North Street is a highly-rated nursery and primary school. The original Blue School building – the Old Blue School – is located in Lower Square and is now apartments. It was one of the oldest Church of England schools in the country, founded in 1630 as the Dame Elizabeth Ellis School for Girls. A charity school, it became known as the Blue School in the 18th century due to the colour of its uniforms. The original Blue School moved to a new site north of London Road at the end of the 19th century and developed into today's Isleworth & Syon School – though it's now a boys' school.

Continue west along South Street, the 'high street' of Old Isleworth, and turn right on Twickenham Road at the end, where the Catholic church of **Our Lady of Sorrows and St Bridget of Sweden** 21 (1909) is on the right. The most celebrated saint of Sweden, Saint Birgitta (1303-1373) was the founder of the Bridgettine Order of Augustinian nuns and monks, who later founded Syon Abbey. Perhaps due to their influence, even after the Reformation Isleworth remained something of a Catholic stronghold and has an unusually

Food & Drink

5 **Coach and Horses:** This old coaching house is now a Young's pub with an interesting menu; recommended for Sunday lunch (10am-11pm, £).

6 **Garden Kitchen**: The café in the Wyvale Garden Centre, Syon Park serves drinks, snacks and light lunches, plus the inevitable cream tea (9am-6pm, £).

20 **South Street Coffee & Ice Cream Shop:** A nice little place in Shrewsbury Walk in Old Isleworth (10am-5pm, £).

large number of RC churches and schools today.

Some 200m past the church turn left into St John's Road. After around 100m the **Duke of Northumberland's River** **22** crosses beneath the road. Created in the 16th and 17th centuries to provide power for flour mills, the river consists of separate upper and lower artificial watercourses, which are both a distributary of the River Colne and a tributary of the River Crane. Continue along St John's Road, where around 400m further on you come to **St John the Baptist, Isleworth** **23**, built on land donated by the Duke Of Northumberland and consecrated in 1856. The road terminates at London Road – the end of the walk – where Isleworth railway station is a few steps along on the right.

Old Isleworth

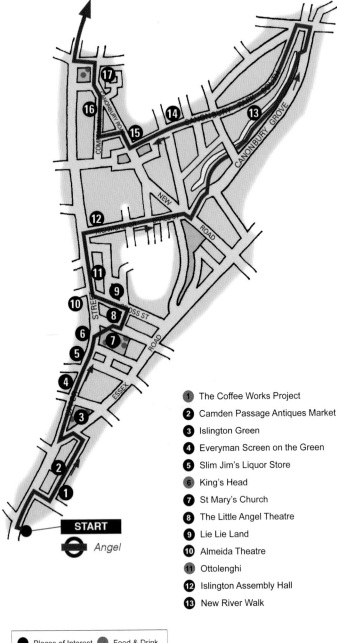

1. The Coffee Works Project
2. Camden Passage Antiques Market
3. Islington Green
4. Everyman Screen on the Green
5. Slim Jim's Liquor Store
6. King's Head
7. St Mary's Church
8. The Little Angel Theatre
9. Lie Lie Land
10. Almeida Theatre
11. Ottolenghi
12. Islington Assembly Hall
13. New River Walk

START

Angel

● Places of Interest ● Food & Drink

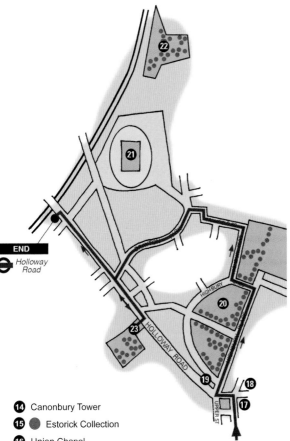

14 Canonbury Tower

15 Estorick Collection

16 Union Chapel

17 Maison d'être

18 Trullo

19 The Garage

20 Highbury Fields

21 Emirates Stadium

22 Gillespie Park & Ecology Centre

23 St Mary Magdalene Church & Gardens

Islington

END
Holloway
Road

Walk 12

Distance: 3½ miles (5½ km)
Terrain: easy, a few hills
Duration: 2 hours
Start: Angel tube
End: Holloway tube
Postcode: N1 9LQ

ISLINGTON

E nergetic, eclectic and just a little bit rough around the edges, Islington in north London is one of the capital's hippest hangouts. From the buzzing retail and entertainment hub of Upper Street to the leafy Georgian squares of Barnsbury and Canonbury, Islington's diverse attractions – handsome terraces, peaceful parks, tempting shops, cool cafés, happening nightlife and some of the finest restaurants in London – lure people from all walks of life.

In the 11th century the Anglo-Saxon name for Islington was Giseldone or Gislandune, meaning 'Gīsla's hill'. Isledon, as it later became, was one of a number of small manors, along with Bernersbury (Barnsbury), Hey-bury (Highbury) and Canonesbury (Canonbury). By the Middle Ages it was a popular residential area, offering easy access to the City and Westminster, and its appeal was further enhanced with the construction of the New River watercourse in the early 1600s.

During the 1800s Islington's landscape was transformed by a surge in property development and the coming of the North London Railway. But it fell out of favour in the 20th century and it wasn't until the '80s that widespread gentrification transformed its streets, attracting the attention of champagne socialists – not for nothing is it dubbed the 'Socialist Republic of Islington'.

Today, Islington is effortlessly fashionable; one of London's most heterogeneous neighbourhoods where all the city's tribes – from celebrities, creatives and upwardly-mobile professionals to hipsters, hustlers and housewives – manage to co-exist. For all its aspirations, Islington has a strong sense of community and is still a village at heart.

Camden Passage

Start Walking…

Our walk begins at Angel tube station, which gets its name from a 17th-century coaching inn which once stood here. Turn right up Islington High Street and bear right after Duncan Street, then left to re-join the high street. The building on the left dates from 1850 and was once a tram shed. **The Coffee Works Project ❶**, on the right, brews an excellent espresso.

The street leads into Camden Passage, an 18th-century, cobblestoned alley running along the backs of the houses on Upper Street. As well as a variety of antiques shops, pubs, cafés and restaurants housed in elegant Georgian buildings, it's also home to the **Camden Passage Antiques Market ❷** which trades on Wednesdays and Saturdays. The market offers a variety of stalls, selling a diverse mix of antiques and collectibles – vintage clothes, handbags, jewellery, silver, porcelain, glass and assorted bric-a-brac.

Sir Hugh Myddleton

A Welsh cloth-maker, entrepreneur, mine-owner, goldsmith, banker and self-taught engineer, Myddleton (1560-1631) was the royal jeweller to James I and MP for Denbigh Boroughs in Wales from 1603 to 1628. He was the driving force behind the ambitious construction of the New River between 1609 and 1613, conceived to bring clean water from the River Lea in Hertfordshire to London. You follow part of the course of the river later on the walk.

Around two-thirds of the way along the passage – just before the Camden Head pub – turn left into Camden Walk and cross the road to **Islington Green ❸**. There's a fine contemporary war memorial here by John Maine (2007) and – at the southern end – John Thomas' marble statue (1862) of Sir Hugh Myddleton (see box, left). From here, turn right and head north on Upper Street, Islington's main thoroughfare: this was once home to left-wing bookshops and squatters' cafés, but they've long been replaced by chichi boutiques, bars and eateries.

Everyman Screen on the Green

Walk 12

St Mary's Church

founded in 1970, it was the first pub theatre to be established in England since Shakespeare's time.

Opposite the King's Head is **St Mary's Church** ❼, a site of worship since the 12th century. The 'current' church was built in 1751-4, although it was largely destroyed during the Blitz (only the tower and spire survived) and the replacement dates from 1954-6. The churchyard is now a public garden. Just past the church, a pathway leads to Dagmar Passage and **The**

Just past the green on the left of Upper Street is the **Everyman Screen on the Green** ❹, an iconic London cinema, while opposite is Fox on the Green, one of Islington's oldest pubs. A few hundred metres up on the right is the renowned Angel Studios, housed in the former Islington Chapel (1888, Grade II listed), where Adele recorded her album *21*. Almost opposite is **Slim Jim's Liquor Store** ❺, which dubs itself 'the UK's first LA-style dive bar' and serenades drinkers with heavy rock. A little further on is the **King's Head** ❻, a handsome Victorian hostelry (1860). There's been a pub on this site since the 16th century, as noted in Samuel Pepys's diaries. The name reputedly refers to Henry VIII who (it's said) would stop here for refreshment en route to see one of his mistresses (although he must have had more mistresses than wives, as it's one of the most common pub names in the country!). The King's Head also hosts London's oldest pub theatre;

New River Walk

By common consent, this magical watery park is one of the loveliest stretches of the New River Path. The tree-shaded tarmac path through the landscaped gardens follows the lovely watercourse (albeit restored and not the original river), which is a haven for wildlife. The path is landscaped with native English plants and specimen trees, including swamp cypress, dawn redwood and graceful weeping willows. The narrow path winds intriguingly and leads over the watercourse at New Bridge Road via an old stone bridge (near the Marquess Tavern – an award-winning gastropub), while further on you cross over an ornamental wooden bridge with a fountain on the right, and there's another grander fountain further on in a large pool. A genuine oasis!

Little Angel Theatre ❽ (1961) – self-proclaimed home of British puppetry. Carry on down the passage to Cross Street. On a wall opposite in Shillingford Street is **Lie Lie Land** ❾ by graffiti artist Bambi, depicting Theresa May dancing with Donald Trump in a pose made famous by the film *La La Land*. Turn left down Cross Street to rejoin Upper Street. Opposite is Almeida Street, home to the **Almeida Theatre** ❿ , a 325-seat studio theatre with an international reputation. Turn right to pass the legendary **Ottolenghi** ⓫ , one of the Mediterranean deli chain's few 'proper' café-restaurants, seating some 50 diners at communal tables.

Islington Assembly Hall

Around 200m further on is the **Islington Assembly Hall** ⓬ , on the corner of Richmond Grove, where you turn right. Opened in 1930, the Art Deco hall was a popular venue for tea dances and variety shows; now restored, it's one of the capital's most exciting live music venues. Continue along Richmond Grove into Braes Street and turn right at the end onto Canonbury Road and then left into Canonbury Grove (just before the Myddleton Arms pub). A little way up on the left is the entrance to the **New River Walk** ⓭ (8am to dusk – see box, left), part of the New River Path that follows the route (28mi/45km) of the New River.

At the end of the New River Walk turn left on St Paul's Road and left again on Canonbury Park North, then bear left almost immediately to Canonbury Park South. Canonbury, which gets its name from the Augustinian canons of St Bartholomew's Priory in Clerkenwell, has one of Islington's oldest buildings, **Canonbury Tower** ⓮ , on the corner of Canonbury Place and Alwyne Villas. It's a well-preserved Tudor structure dating from the early 1500s, in the reign of Henry VII, and was once part of a manor house with a long and interesting history. Its residents have included Thomas Cromwell, who was given Canonbury in 1539 by Henry VIII (just a year before he was executed for treason); Sir John Spencer, sometime Lord Mayor of London, who occupied it from 1570 to 1610; and author, philosopher and statesman Sir Francis Bacon, who lived there for nine years. Just around the corner from the tower, in Alwyne Villas, is handsome Canonbury House, once part of the manor house and rebuilt in around 1770.

Some 100m past the tower you reach Canonbury Square. Dating from 1800, it's one of the capital's most beautiful squares; former residents include writers Evelyn Waugh and George Orwell, and it's now home to the **Estorick Collection** ⓯ (entrance fee, see box, page 114) and its lovely café.

From the museum continue north on Canonbury Road and turn left into Edward's Cottages and right on Compton Avenue, where on the left is the **Union Chapel** . Built in 1877, the chapel is a vibrant community hub and award-winning venue that's a combination of working church, performance space and homeless shelter. This architectural treasure (Grade II listed) is noted for its breathtaking Gothic interior, fantastic acoustics and superb organ (made by Henry Willis). Behind the chapel is Compton Terrace and Gardens, designed by Henry Leroux, with a row of villas either side of the chapel completed in 1830.

Soon after the chapel you're briefly back on Canonbury Road before arriving at busy Highbury Corner. On the right is **Maison d'être** , a delightful little independent coffee house, while just off to the right on the other side of St Paul's Road is the superb **Trullo** , an Italian restaurant with flavoursome food, friendly service, nice ambience and good value. Walk around the island anticlockwise to Highbury Corner where, after 50m or so, is **The Garage** , one of the city's best club-sized indie and rock venues. Retrace your steps to Highbury Place and turn left to reach the corner with Highbury Crescent and a fine Art Nouveau Boer War memorial (1905) by Bertram McKennal, featuring a wreath, cannons and the captured standards of defeated enemies.

Just behind it is **Highbury Fields** , the largest open space (29 acres/11.75ha) in the borough of Islington; the park is scattered with fine oak, horse chestnut and lime trees, while London planes line its perimeter and principal walks. Highbury Fields is surrounded by elegant Georgian and Victorian townhouses, home to many famous residents over the years, including painter Walter Sickert (number 1 Highbury Place) and statesman Joseph Chamberlain (number 15).

Continue along Highbury Place, turn left on Highbury Crescent and go right along Highbury Terrace (built in 1789), which runs north parallel to the park. At the end

Estorick Collection

A hidden gem housed in a handsome 19th-century house, the Estorick (Wed-Sat 11am-6pm, Sun noon-5pm, closed Mon-Tue) is Britain's only gallery devoted to modern Italian art (including sculpture and figurative art) and it also houses one of the world's best collections of early 20th-century Italian art, particularly the Futurism movement. The collection's title comes from Eric Estorick (1913-1993), an American sociologist, writer and art collector, who left his collection to a charitable foundation. The Grade II listed house was previously the home of architect Sir Basil Spence, and is a fine example of Georgian architecture. (See www.estorickcollection.com for information.)

Highbury Fields

grounds) were transformed into a public park at the close of the 19th century; with a wealth of majestic trees, they are a lovely place to chill out. Leave the church and turn left to head back along Holloway Road to the tube station and the end of the walk.

go left on Framfield Road and continue to the end, taking the walkway through to Whistler Street and following it round to the right to reach Drayton Park. Over on the right, the **Emirates Stadium** ㉑ looms large; it's been the home of Arsenal Football Club since 2006, when the club moved from its old Highbury Stadium (now converted into flats). Just north of the Emirates on Drayton Park is the **Gillespie Park & Ecology Centre** ㉒, a 7-acre (2.8ha) Local Nature Reserve created in 1983 on the site of the Great Northern Railway sidings. The park contains a remarkable diversity of habitats, including woodland, meadow and ponds, and is home to an abundance of wildlife, including many rare species.

For now, turn left along Drayton Park, passing the railway station on your right, to Holloway Road. Turn left and around 200m along on the right is **St Mary Magdalene Church & Gardens** ㉓. The church is a handsome, early 19th-century (1814) neo-classical chapel of ease. The gardens (originally the church burial

Food & Drink

- ① **The Coffee Works Project:** Independent speciality coffee house on Camden Passage (7.30am-6pm, £).

- ⑥ **King's Head:** Modern theatre pub on Upper Street, offering fine ales and good pub grub (11am-11pm, £).

- ⑪ **Ottolenghi**: Yotam's Upper Street deli, open for breakfast, lunch and dinner – and a legendary weekend brunch (8am-10.30pm, £).

- ⑮ **Estorick Caffè:** The Estorick Museum's licensed Italian café with a beautiful landscaped garden (Wed-Sun 11am-6pm, closed Mon-Tue, £).

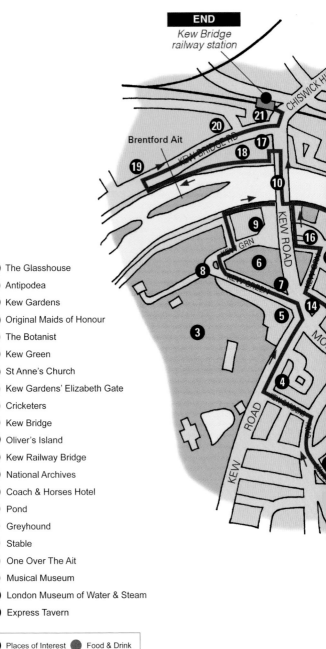

END
Kew Bridge
railway station

CHISWICK HIG

Brentford Ait

KEW BRIDGE RD

KEW ROAD

GRN

FISHER'S

KEW ROAD

MO

1. The Glasshouse
2. Antipodea
3. Kew Gardens
4. Original Maids of Honour
5. The Botanist
6. Kew Green
7. St Anne's Church
8. Kew Gardens' Elizabeth Gate
9. Cricketers
10. Kew Bridge
11. Oliver's Island
12. Kew Railway Bridge
13. National Archives
14. Coach & Horses Hotel
15. Pond
16. Greyhound
17. Stable
18. One Over The Ait
19. Musical Museum
20. London Museum of Water & Steam
21. Express Tavern

● Places of Interest ● Food & Drink

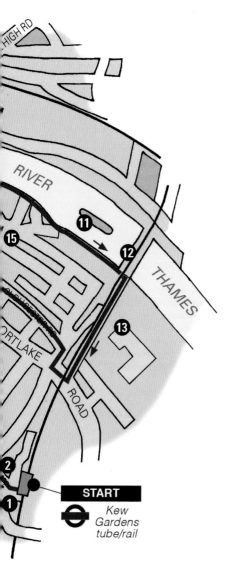

START

Kew
Gardens
tube/rail

Kew

Walk 13

Distance: 3 miles (5 km)
Terrain: easy, mostly flat
Duration: 1½ hours
Start: Kew Gardens rail/tube
End: Kew Bridge rail
Postcode: TW9 3BZ

KEW

One of the most attractive corners of southwest London and a close neighbour to elegant Richmond-upon-Thames, Kew is best known for its world-famous gardens, its lovely green and for being the home of the National Archives. But its charming compact village merits a visit, too, for its fine Georgian and Victorian architecture, sweeping Thames river frontage, and some outstanding restaurants, cafés and pubs.

The name Kew is derived from two words: the Old French *kai* (or quay) and Old English *hoh* (a 'spur of land') formed in this case by a bend in the Thames. Its first documented namecheck appeared in the 14th century, when it was recorded in 1327 as Cayho (among other spellings), although Kew didn't become a parish in its own right until the 1700s. The area has a long association with royalty. Henry V founded a Carthusian monastery in 1414 to the southwest of where the King's Observatory now stands in the Old Deer Park in Richmond. And Queen Anne donated land for the parish church on Kew Green, which was dedicated to St Anne in 1714, three months before the queen's death.

The Hanoverians maintained the strongest links with Kew, in particular Princess Augusta, Dowager Princess of Wales (widow of Frederick, Prince of Wales). She founded the botanic gardens at Kew in 1759, although they had their roots in the exotic garden at Kew Park, home of the Capel family, in the latter half of the 17th century. Augusta and Frederick lived at the White House in Kew (which stood in front of today's Kew Palace), while Prince George, later George II, moved into Richmond Lodge at the south end of what is now Kew Gardens. Later, the future George III and Queen Charlotte lived in the White House and established their main summer court at Kew in the 1760s-1770s.

Modern Kew developed in the late 19th century after the arrival of the railway in 1869 and the District Line (Underground) in 1877. Further development took place in the '20s and '30s when new houses were built on the market gardens of North Sheen. Today, Kew is an upmarket residential area, popular for its fine architecture, riverside location, open spaces and greenery, low-rise skyline, good schools, convenient transport links, and quality independent shops, restaurants and gastropubs. Our walk takes you around its highlights, from the village to the green, ending up just over the river at Kew Bridge.

Start Walking…

On leaving Kew Gardens station, you immediately find yourself in the heart of Kew Village; its centre is formed by the triangle of Station Parade, Sandycombe Road and Station Approach where there's an attractive range of independent shops, restaurants, cafés and pubs. The area in front

Kew Gardens

The Royal Botanic Gardens, Kew – better known simply as Kew Gardens (see website below for opening times) – comprise around 300 acres (121ha) of gardens and botanical glasshouses. Created in 1759, the gardens welcome some 2 million visitors annually, and have been a UNESCO World Heritage Site since 2003. They contain some 50,000 plants from throughout the world, including over 14,000 trees, while the Herbarium has over 7 million specimens. The gardens also contain six magnificent glasshouses, where tropical and sub-tropical plants are kept in climatic conditions. Kew's rich horticultural and scientific history – it houses the world's largest and most diverse botanical collections – is interwoven with its royal heritage and historical importance. You don't need to be a gardener to enjoy Kew. (See www.kew.org for information.)

of the station is the venue for lively Kew Village Market on the first Sunday of each month (see http://kewvillagemarket.org). On the left on Station Parade is the award-winning Michelin-starred restaurant **The Glasshouse** ❶, where chef Berwyn Davies conjures up delicious international cuisine. Immediately on the right on Station Approach is

Kew Gardens

Walk 13

Oliver's, an award-winning neighbourhood wholefoods store (est. 1989), offering the best organic produce from small, local producers. If you missed breakfast or fancy a coffee, **Antipodea** ② is a superb Aussie all-day café/brasserie just past Oliver's.

Original Maids of Honour

At the end of Station Approach, go right on Kew Gardens Road and follow it round to **Kew Gardens** ③ (see box, page 119). The gardens aren't included in this walk – it takes a day (or a week!) to explore them and entry costs £17 for an adult, £5 for a child (a bit less online). Turn right along Kew Road – where there are many grand period homes facing the gardens – and around 200m along is the **Original Maids of Honour**, ④ a charming traditional bakery and teashop steeped in history. Housed in an attractive '40s mock Tudor building (the original Victorian building was destroyed in WWII), the teashop takes its name from the delicious cakes that allegedly took Henry VIII's fancy (that wasn't all that took his fancy!) when he discovered Anne Boleyn and the other Maids of Honour scoffing them at Richmond Palace.

Continue along Kew Road to its junction with the South Circular Road, where **The Botanist** ⑤ on the corner of Kew Green beckons – a gem of a gastropub serving cask ales and seasonal food.

Just past the Botanist turn left along **Kew Green** ⑥. At 30 acres (12ha) and roughly triangular in shape, the green consists of open grassland, framed with broadleaf trees, bordered by handsome 18th and 19th-century townhouses; there's also the obligatory cricket pitch and pond. Situated in the southeast corner of the green is **St Anne's Church** ⑦. The original church was a tiny chapel, built in 1714, although it has been enlarged and much altered since; its website (http://saintanne-kew.org.uk/kew-green) contains a

St Anne's Church

graphic illustration of how it has evolved over the years. The churchyard has some significant graves and tombs, including those of painters Thomas Gainsborough, Johann Zoffany and George Engelheart, known for his portrait miniatures, while notable figures from the botanic world include William Aiton, the first director of Kew Gardens, and his son William Townsend Aiton who succeeded him in the role.

On the south side of the green, numbers 33 (King's Cottage) and 37 (Cambridge Cottage) are fine 18th-century townhouses, while Sir William Hooker and his son Sir Joseph lived at number 49 – the official residence of the director of Kew Gardens – shown by a blue plaque above the covered garden path. A bit further along – just past number 57 before the road loops round to the right – is **Kew Gardens' Elizabeth Gate** ❽. Continue around Kew Green, past Ferry Lane, to see more attractive period houses along the northern edge. One worthy of mention is early 18th-century Capel House (no 83), which is next door to the **Cricketers** ❾ (yet another fine pub) on the corner of Bush Road.

Retrace your steps to Ferry Lane, where you pass Kew Green Preparatory School, to the Thames Path. Here the route goes right, although you may wish to explore the attractive path to the left, which runs parallel to Ferry Lane for around 400m; there's a distant view of 17th-century Kew Palace from the pathway. Continuing along the Thames Path in an easterly direction you pass under **Kew Bridge** ❿; the third bridge on this site, it was designed by Sir John Wolfe Barry and Cuthbert A. Brereton, and

The National Archives

The guardian of many of the country's most iconic national documents dating back over 1,000 years, the National Archives (Tue-Sat, 9am-5/7pm, free entry) are accessible to anyone aged 14 or over. The interactive museum showcases some of the diverse treasures of the archives, which range from the Magna Carta to Jane Austen's will and the *Domesday Book*. There's an excellent bookshop and café, too. (See www.nationalarchives.gov.uk for information.)

built in 1903. Beyond the bridge is Westerly Ware Park – the name refers to the practice of netting weirs or 'wares' to catch fish – a small memorial garden and recreation ground. On the embankment alongside the park is Kew Pier; ferries leave here between late March and October, sailing to Richmond, Hampton Court and Westminster Pier. There's a fine view from here of Strand-on-the-Green on the opposite side of the Thames.

A few hundred metres past the park is **Oliver's Island** ⓫, an eyot (a small island in a river)

Kew Green

named after Oliver Cromwell, who made his temporary headquarters at a local inn during the Civil War. Just past the island is the elegant pale green **Kew Railway Bridge** 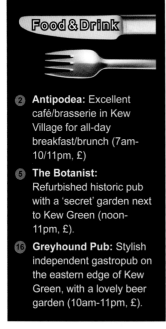⑫ , opened in 1869, after which you turn inland on a footpath leading to the **National Archives** ⑬ (see box, page 121), the official archive of the UK government and of England and Wales.

Food & Drink

- ② **Antipodea:** Excellent café/brasserie in Kew Village for all-day breakfast/brunch (7am-10/11pm, £)

- ⑤ **The Botanist:** Refurbished historic pub with a 'secret' garden next to Kew Green (noon-11pm, £).

- ⑯ **Greyhound Pub:** Stylish independent gastropub on the eastern edge of Kew Green, with a lovely beer garden (10am-11pm, £).

The footpath terminates at Mortlake Road, where you go right and right again into Forest Road (avoiding the traffic-choked South Circular Road), then left along Gloucester Road to return to the eastern edge of Kew Green. On the left is the grand **Coach**

& Horses Hotel ⑭ , Kew's oldest inn and now a gastropub. Go right along the edge of the green, where you pass Haverfield House (no 24), named after John Haverfield who managed the Kew Royal Estates in the 18th century; pre-Raphaelite painter Arthur Hughes lived next door at number 22 from 1858 to 1915. Continue along the green to the northeastern corner, where the **Pond** ⑮ is believed to date from the 10th century, and is thought to have originally been a natural pond fed from a creek of the tidal Thames. During high (spring) tides, sluice gates are opened to allow river water to fill the pond via an underground channel. It's been partly concreted over but still provides an important reed bed habitat vital for conservation and resident water birds.

Follow the green round to the left – past more handsome period houses – and you come to the **Greyhound** ⑯ , a pub renowned for its tasty food, particularly Sunday roasts, and lovely garden. Just before the South Circular go right along the footpath to Westerly Ware Park, past the Legends Boxing Gym on the left, cross under the road and

Greyhound

go up the stairs to Kew Bridge, and cross to the north bank of the Thames.

We are now in Brentford, but we won't let that spoil our walk! Around 100m over the bridge, take the stairs down to Kew Road, next to a modern building housing the **Stable** ⑰ chain restaurant, and go left to the Thames Path. Walk along the path – where the bank is lined with barges – passing **One Over The Ait** ⑱ , a Fuller's pub in a Victorian warehouse. The pub's name is a nod to Brentford Ait, the long uninhabited island in the river here that was home to a notorious pub called the Swan or Three Swans in the 18th century. At the 'end' of the riverside path, just past O'Riordans pub and before Watermans Park, go right and cross over the High Street to the **Musical Museum** ⑲ (Tue, Fri-Sun, 11am-5pm, entrance fee, www.musicalmuseum.co.uk). Founded in 1963 by Frank Holland (1910-1989), this unique purpose-built museum contains one of the world's largest collections of mechanical musical instruments; there's also a pleasant tearoom and a fascinating shop.

Walk along the High Street back towards the bridge, where around 300m up on the left is the absorbing **London Museum of Water & Steam** ⑳ (11am-4pm, entrance fee, see box, right). From the museum, go left along the High Street, passing the **Express Tavern** ㉑ , a CAMRA award-winning pub, to Kew Bridge railway station, and the end of the walk.

London Museum of Water & Steam

This unique museum (est. 1975) tells the story of London's water supply – from Roman times to the present day – and houses a magnificent collection of steam engines and diesel-powered water pumping machines. It's housed within the Georgian and Italianate buildings of the former Kew Bridge Pumping Station – opened in 1838 by the Grand Junction Waterworks Company – which supplied west Londoners with water for over 100 years until the engines were retired in 1944. The museum is home to the world's largest collection of Cornish beam engines, including the largest working beam engine, the spectacular Grand Junction 90 Engine that pumped water for 98 years. It also features London's only operating steam railway, and has a café and a pleasant garden for picnics. (See www.waterandsteam.org.uk for more information.)

1 St George's Cathedral
2 Tibetan Peace Garden
3 Imperial War Museum
4 Newport Street Gallery
5 Garden Museum
6 Lambeth Palace
7 Lambeth Bridge
8 St Thomas' Hospital
9 Florence Nightingale Museum
10 Westminster Bridge
11 South Bank Lion
12 County Hall
13 London Eye
14 Jubilee Gardens
15 Southbank Centre
16 Waterloo Bridge
17 Southbank Centre Book Market
18 National Theatre
19 Gabriel's Wharf
20 Oxo Tower
21 Anchor & Hope
22 Union Jack Club
23 Waterloo Station
24 Old Vic
25 Lower Marsh Market
26 Scooter Caffè

THA

RIVER

YORK ROAD

WESTM

WESTM

LAMBETH PALACE ROAD

LAM

● Places of Interest ● Food & Drink

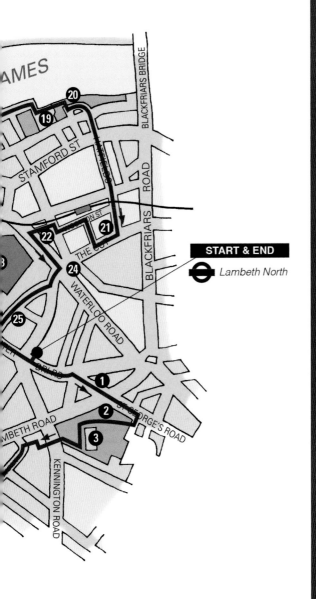

START & END
Lambeth North

WALK 14

Lambeth

Distance: 3½ miles (5½ km)
Terrain: easy, mostly flat
Duration: 2 hours
Start/End: Lambeth North tube
Postcode: SE1 7XG

LAMBETH

Home to an archbishops' palace, an acclaimed arts complex and some fascinating museums, historic Lambeth sits on the south bank of the River Thames. Originally part of the ancient parish of Lambeth St Mary, the site of Lambeth Palace, its name was recorded in 1062 as Lambehitha ('landing place for lambs'). One of the first records of the area is in the *Domesday Book* of 1086, referring to the local manor closest to the City of London; records show that it was owned by the Archbishop of Canterbury from at least 1190.

Lambeth Marsh first appeared in historical records in 1377 and is one of the oldest settlements on the south bank, possibly dating back to Roman times. Until the early 19th century, north Lambeth was mostly marshland surrounded by open fields, crossed by roads raised against floods. The marshlands were drained in the 18th century, but are remembered in the Lower Marsh street name. Two streets, Lower Marsh and The Cut, formed the commercial heart of the area from the early 19th century, when they had an unsavoury reputation.

Waterloo Station was built in 1848 and completely changed the character of Lambeth, with the huge railway station creating a barrier between Lower Marsh, the river and the rest of Lambeth Marsh. The area around the station soon became known as Waterloo and by 1860 – as London expanded and became increasingly industrialised – Lambeth Marsh village was subsumed into the town of Lambeth. Previously part of Surrey, Lambeth became a London borough in 1889.

Lower Marsh – now a conservation area – underwent gentrification in the late 20th century and is now at the heart of a vibrant neighbourhood, the site of Lower Marsh Market and a range of vintage shops, pubs, galleries and eateries. It's one of the highlights

Lambeth

of the walk, which also takes in some of Lambeth's many Thameside attractions, from the Garden Museum to the Oxo Tower.

Start Walking…

From Lambeth North tube station turn left along Westminster Bridge Road, passing the Lincoln Tower, a landmark spire (1876) with unusual Stars and Stripes brickwork; it was donated by the family of President Abraham Lincoln. A short way on is Morley College, founded in the 1880s, while just across St George's Road is majestic **St George's Cathedral ❶**. A Gothic Revival Roman Catholic cathedral consecrated in 1848, St George's was designed by Augustus Pugin (1812-1852), famous for his work with Charles Barry on the Palace of Westminster. Sadly, Pugin spent some of his last days in the building opposite the church: the former Bethlem Royal Hospital (or Bedlam as the psychiatric hospital was known).

Cross Lambeth Road and St George's Road to reach Geraldine Mary Harmsworth Park, which opened in 1934 on land that was gifted to the 'splendid struggling mothers of Southwark' by Harold

Harmsworth, 1st Viscount Rothermere, and named after his mother. In the northeast corner is the **Tibetan Peace Garden ❷** or *Samten Kyil*, a beautiful tranquil oasis designed by Hamish Horsley, who also created many of the garden's sculptures. In complete (and incongruous) contrast, the park is also home to the **Imperial War Museum ❸** (free entry, café) which occupies the old Bethlem buildings (1815). Founded in 1917, it's the world's leading authority on conflict and its impact with an absorbing collection, although you'll need several hours for just a cursory inspection of the exhibits.

Imperial War Museum

Leave the museum and park via the western exit on Kennington Road, cross over to China Walk and follow it round to Lambeth Walk. Turn left and continue along the road which inspired the famous '30s song *The Lambeth Walk*. This, along with Lambeth High Street, was one of Lambeth's principal commercial streets before World War Two. On your left is a variety of distinguished establishments, including the redbrick Pelham Hall Sculpture

Tibetan Peace Garden

Garden Museum

The museum (entrance fee) occupies the building and churchyard of the deconsecrated church of St Mary-at-Lambeth, dating from the 14th century. The museum was established to rescue the church from demolition following the discovery of the graves of two 17th-century royal gardeners and plant hunters, John Tradescant (father and son). Anne Boleyn's mother Elizabeth also rests here, as does William Bligh, captain of the infamous *Bounty*. It was the world's first museum dedicated to the history of gardening, and celebrates British gardens and gardening through its collection, temporary exhibitions, events, symposia and garden.

Studio, violin-maker Ballard Violins and the Poetry School.

Around 150m past the school turn right down Old Paradise Street, where a short distance along on the left is **Newport Street Gallery** ④ (free admission), a showcase for Damien Hirst's art collection. At the end of the street turn right on Lambeth High Street to Lambeth Road, and cross over to the **Garden Museum** ⑤ (see box, above) and the Garden Café opposite.

Next door to the museum is Morton's Tower (1490), the gatehouse that guards the entrance to **Lambeth Palace** ⑥ , London residence of the Archbishops of Canterbury since the 12th century. The palace and its gardens aren't open to the public but guided tours can be booked via its website (www.archbishopofcanterbury.org/pages/visit-lambeth-palace.html). From Morton's Tower cross over to the Albert Embankment alongside the Thames, which was constructed in the 19th century to house part of the city's sewer system. From here you have a good view of **Lambeth Bridge** ⑦ , opened in 1932 and painted red to match the colour of the seats in the House of Lords (Westminster Bridge, further downstream, is painted green to match the seats in the Commons).

Turn right and walk north along the embankment, past the imposing Victorian buildings of **St Thomas' Hospital** ⑧ , opposite the Palace of Westminster. One of London's most famous teaching hospitals, it was named after St Thomas Becket and founded in the 12th century at Borough (Southwark), though it has been based in Lambeth since 1871. Designed by Henry Currey, the original 1868 hospital buildings are

Lambeth Palace

Florence Nightingale Museum

This collection (entrance fee) tells the engrossing story of one of Britain's greatest heroines. From the slate she used as a child to the Turkish lantern she carried in the Crimean War – which earned her the sobriquet 'the Lady with the Lamp' – the museum spans Florence Nightingale's (1820-1910) life and nursing legacy. She was a visionary health reformer, brilliant campaigner and the second most influential woman in Victorian Britain after Queen Victoria. The Nightingale Pledge, taken by new nurses, is named in her honour, and International Nurses Day is still celebrated on her birthday (12th May).

and restaurants, plus the London Aquarium and London Dungeon. On the river is the landmark Coca-Cola **London Eye** ❸ (see box).

In the shadow of the London Eye, **Jubilee Gardens** ❹ was created to celebrate the Queen's Silver Jubilee in 1977 and redeveloped for her Diamond Jubilee in 2012. One of its highlights is a striking memorial to the casualties of the International Brigades of the Spanish Civil War. Leave the park on the river side and walk under Hungerford Bridge (and the Golden Jubilee foot bridges) to emerge in front of the **Southbank Centre** ❺, Europe's

best admired from the northern bank of the Thames. Just past the hospital is a small garden, behind which is the **Florence Nightingale Museum** ❾ (see box, above).

Continuing along the embankment, go under **Westminster Bridge** ❿, designed by Thomas Page and constructed in 1862, making it the oldest road bridge in central London. Above the embankment on the north side of Westminster Bridge Road is the magnificent Coade artificial stone **South Bank Lion** ⓫, originally made for the local Lion Brewery (which closed in 1924) and installed here in 1966. Past the bridge the embankment becomes The Queen's Walk, where the first building you see is the old **County Hall** ⓬, former London County Council HQ, which now houses a hotel, offices, shops

London Eye

A giant 'Ferris' wheel, the London Eye opened in March 2000 to celebrate the start of the new millennium and quickly became one of the capital's most iconic sights. The wheel stands 443ft (135m) tall with a diameter of 394ft (120m) and is Europe's tallest observation wheel, with 32 10-tonne capsules each holding up to 25 people. On a clear day you can see for up to 25 miles (40km).

Westminster Bridge

Walk 14

River Thames & Gabriel's Wharf

largest centre for the arts. Opened in 1951, it houses a complex of artistic venues, including the Royal Festival Hall, the Queen Elizabeth Hall and the Hayward Gallery, as well as a number of bars and restaurants. The next bridge along is **Waterloo Bridge** ⑯, designed by Sir Giles Gilbert Scott and opened in 1942, where the **Southbank Centre Book Market** ⑰ is held daily.

Just past the bridge is the **National Theatre** ⑱, opened in 1963 and one of the UK's leading performing arts venues. Some 200m further on you come to **Gabriel's Wharf** ⑲, which encompasses an eclectic mix of boutiques – many owned and run by artists and designers – cafés, bars and restaurants, and the green oasis of Bernie Spain Gardens, named after a local community campaigner, Bernadette Spain. Overlooking the river, the iconic **Oxo Tower** ⑳ (see box, right) has a rooftop viewing gallery open to the public, as well as the acclaimed Oxo Tower restaurant, bar and brasserie, operated by Harvey Nichols.

Just before the Oxo Tower take Barge House Street, cross Stamford Street and go down Hatfields (under the railway line) – yes, they used to make hats here – to The Cut, where you turn right. If you're hungry this is a good place to refuel; on the corner is the **Anchor & Hope** ㉑, a celebrated no-frills gastropub. Carry on up The Cut, passing the Young Vic Theatre and the Windmill Tavern on your right, and turn right along

Oxo Tower

A former power station, the tower was acquired in the '20s by the Liebig Extract of Meat Company, manufacturers of Oxo beef stock cubes, for conversion into a cold store. Between 1928 and 1929 it was largely rebuilt in an Art Deco design by company architect Albert Moore. Liebig wanted to include a tower featuring illuminated signs advertising the Oxo name; when permission was refused they built the tower with four sets of three vertically-aligned windows, each of which was 'coincidentally' in the shapes of a circle, a cross and a circle spelling OXO! Now refurbished, the tower is a splendid sight at night when the letters are illuminated in red.

Windmill Walk to Wootton Street. Turn left down Wootton Street to Cornwall Road – opposite is the **Union Jack Club** 22 , an armed forces club founded over 100 years ago – and right down Sandell Street to Waterloo Road. Facing you is **Waterloo Station** 23 , named after the battle in which the Duke of Wellington (et al) defeated Napoleon in 1815.

Turn left and continue along Waterloo Road to Waterloo Green – the famous **Old Vic** 24 theatre (1818) is opposite on the corner of The Cut – where you turn right on Baylis Road and second right into Lower Marsh. This is the beating heart of old Lambeth, where Lambeth Marsh village once stood; along with The Cut, Lower Marsh has been preserved as a conservation area and, remarkably, still manages to retain a village-like atmosphere in the shadow of Waterloo Station. Today, the vibrant street is famous for the **Lower Marsh Market** 25 , a weekday street food market and Saturday flea and crafts market. Among the wealth of independent shops on Lower Marsh are the superb La Barca Ristorante (Italian restaurant), the Four Corners (chic coffee shop), Greensmiths (independent artisan supermarket), the Camel & Artichoke (cosy 18th-century pub with beer garden), and the **Scooter Caffè** 26 , which is a great little coffee shop by day and a buzzy bar in the evening.

At the end of Lower Marsh turn left into Westminster Bridge Road and after 200m or so, you're back where you started at Lambeth

North tube station and the end of the walk.

Food & Drink

⑤ **Garden Café**: Highly rated café at the Garden Museum serving seasonal food; lunch from noon-3pm (2pm Sat) and dinner (Tue and Fri only) from 6-10pm (8am-5pm, Sat 9am-3.30pm, Sun 9am-5pm, £).

⑳ **Oxo Tower Brasserie:** Upmarket restaurant, brasserie and bar on top of the Oxo Tower, with superb views – try the exquisite afternoon tea (noon-11pm, ££).

㉑ **Anchor & Hope:** Superb no-frills gastropub on The Cut, offering a wide selection of ales (11am-11pm, 12.30-3.15pm Sun, 5-11pm Mon, £).

㉖ **Scooter Caffè:** Hip little café on Lower Marsh serving excellent coffee and cakes (8.30am-11pm/midnight, £).

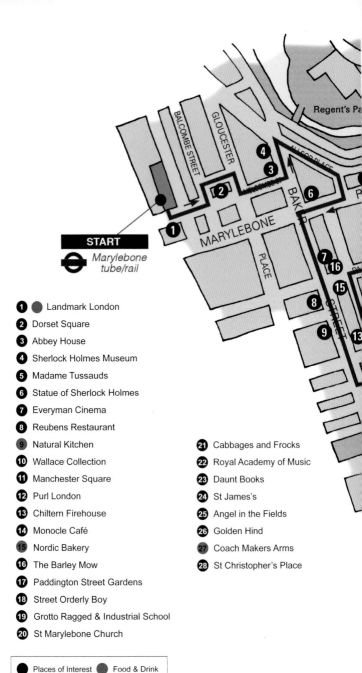

START

Marylebone tube/rail

1. Landmark London
2. Dorset Square
3. Abbey House
4. Sherlock Holmes Museum
5. Madame Tussauds
6. Statue of Sherlock Holmes
7. Everyman Cinema
8. Reubens Restaurant
9. Natural Kitchen
10. Wallace Collection
11. Manchester Square
12. Purl London
13. Chiltern Firehouse
14. Monocle Café
15. Nordic Bakery
16. The Barley Mow
17. Paddington Street Gardens
18. Street Orderly Boy
19. Grotto Ragged & Industrial School
20. St Marylebone Church
21. Cabbages and Frocks
22. Royal Academy of Music
23. Daunt Books
24. St James's
25. Angel in the Fields
26. Golden Hind
27. Coach Makers Arms
28. St Christopher's Place

Places of Interest   Food & Drink

Marylebone

Distance: 2½ miles (4 km)
Terrain: easy
Duration: 1½ hours
Start: Marylebone tube/rail
End: Bond Street tube
Postcode: NW1 6JJ

MARYLEBONE

Prized for its lovely Georgian residences and swanky shops, Marylebone has a unique village charm which belies its close proximity to the frenetic West End. The medieval village of Marylebone takes its name from a church dedicated to St Mary which stood on the banks of a small stream or 'bourne' called the Tybourne – the old name for the River Tyburn which flows underground from Hampstead to the Thames. The church and surrounding area became known as St Mary at the Bourne, which over time became shortened to St Mary-le-Bourne and, eventually, Marylebone.

The manor of Tyburn is mentioned in the *Domesday Book* (1086) as a possession of Barking Abbey, when it had a population no greater than 50 and a value of 52 shillings! In the 16th century it was owned by Henry VIII who hunted deer there. The fortunes of the area improved dramatically in the 18th century when parts of the manor were developed by wealthy landowners, including the Duke of Newcastle, the Earl of Oxford and the Duke of Portland (who had married into the wealthy Cavendish family). Their involvement is reflected in place names such as Cavendish Square and Portland Place. A large area in the west was developed by the Portman family, known as the Portman Estate (around Portman Square). When the Portland family line ended in 1879, the estate passed to the Howard de Waldens, who still own and manage 92 acres. The fact that much of Marylebone is still owned by aristocratic estates has helped protect it from developers and allowed it to retain its charm and atmosphere.

Now part of the City of Westminster, Marylebone is just a few steps away from the hustle and bustle of Oxford Street, yet remains a surprising oasis of (relative) calm. Distinguished by leafy streets lined with gorgeous Georgian homes and tempting boutiques, it's a true urban village complete with colourful characters and a weekly farmers' market – and a real sense of community. Life centres on the bustling High Street, where independent shops, smart restaurants, chic bars and traditional pubs jostle for attention. This walk, which wends its way from Baker St to Bond St, may well take several hours, particularly if you're tempted by designer stores!

Start Walking…

Our walk begins at Marylebone Station, which opened in 1899 as the London terminus of the Great Central Railway, the last major railway line constructed in London until the Channel Tunnel rail link (HS1) opened in 2003. Exit via the main entrance onto Melcombe Place and opposite is the **Landmark London** ❶ , a 5-star 'palace' opened in 1899 as the Great Central Hotel; it was one of the city's luxurious 19th-century railway hotels, with rooms at three shillings and sixpence a night.

Sherlock Holmes Museum

This museum must be the only one in the world dedicated to a fictional character and housed at an address that shouldn't exist! Although the building lies between numbers 237 and 241, towards the north end of Baker Street, it bears the number 221B, granted by the City of Westminster in 1990. This is to correspond with the stories written by Sir Arthur Conan Doyle, whose famous detective Sherlock Holmes shared accommodation with Dr John Watson at 221B Baker Street between 1881 and 1904. The museum features rooms which look as they would've done during Holmes' and Watson's residence (had they existed).

Prices have increased somewhat since then, but if you're feeling flush treat yourself to breakfast or a coffee in its splendid surroundings.

Go left from the station along Melcombe Place which leads you to **Dorset Square** ❷ , a garden square built on what was the old Lord's Cricket Ground before it moved to its current location in St John's Wood. Go left on Dorset Square (opposite Balcome Street) and walk around the square back to Melcombe Street, where you go left. At the end of the street you come to Baker Street, named after builder William Baker who laid it out in the 18th century. Immediately on the left is **Abbey House** ❸ , the former HQ of the Abbey National Building Society 1932-2002; it now houses

Landmark Hotel

Wallace Collection

One of the finest private art collections in the world, the Wallace Collection was amassed by five generations of the Hertford dynasty – the first four Marquesses of Hertford and the 4th Marquess's illegitimate son, Sir Richard Wallace – and is located in attractive 18th-century (1776) Hertford House on Manchester Square. It's a tremendous assemblage of fine and decorative arts dating from the 15th to 19th centuries, spread over 25 galleries, including French 18th-century paintings, furniture (one of the finest collections of French furniture outside France), Sèvres porcelain, outstanding arms and armour, and Old Master paintings, including Franz Hals' *Laughing Cavalier*.

apartments, but the original façade and clock tower have been retained. Just past Abbey House is the **Sherlock Holmes Museum** ❹ (fee, see box, page 135).

Next door to the museum is the Volunteer, a pub with pavement tables, from where you cross the road and head right along Allsop Place to **Madame Tussauds** ❺ on the left as you join Marylebone Road. This is the original waxworks – now part of a worldwide chain – founded in 1835 by French wax sculptor Marie Tussaud; it's a major tourist attraction but certainly not a cheap thrill (adult tickets cost £35 on the door!) and you need several hours to see the 300 or so waxworks on show. From the museum turn

right along Marylebone Road, passing John Doubleday's **Statue of Sherlock Holmes** ❻, unveiled in 1999 outside Baker Street tube station.

Cross the road and turn left to head south down Baker Street, one of Marylebone's main thoroughfares. Around 150m down on the left is the **Everyman** ❼, a luxurious cinema complete with a café, cocktail bar and lounge, while further along on the right is **Reubens Restaurant** ❽, a traditional kosher restaurant with a bustling upstairs deli – perfect for a takeaway lunch. Or just across Dorset Street is the **Natural Kitchen** ❾, one of London's best food emporiums, offering everything a committed foodie could desire. Around 250m past the Kitchen turn left on George Street and take the first right down Manchester Street to Manchester Square, one of central London's best-preserved Georgian squares. On your left as you enter the square is the **Wallace Collection** ❿ (free entry, see box, left).

From the museum take a circuit around **Manchester Square** ⓫, home to many eminent Londoners over the last few centuries, but now mostly offices. Returning to Manchester Street, cross over George Street and go left on Blandford Street, before taking a right into Chiltern Street. On the corner of Blandford and Chiltern Streets is super-cool basement bar **Purl London** ⓬ – named for an old English drink of warm ale, gin, wormwood and spices – one of the capital's most acclaimed cocktail bars (booking essential).

On the left, occupying a converted neo-Gothic fire station dating from 1889 is the five-star **Chiltern Firehouse Hotel & Restaurant** ⑬, which has received rave reviews since opening in 2013. The sympathetically restored building offers elegant rooms with working fireplaces, and is home to one of the city's most celebrated restaurants, led by Michelin-starred chef Nuno Mendes.

Nordic Bakery

Opposite the Chiltern Firehouse, the **Monocle Café** ⑭ is a strikingly-decorated café – think Swedish sauna meets sushi bar. Opened in 2013, it's a spin-off from *Monocle* magazine, the showcase of design consultant and publisher Tyler Brûlé (who founded *Wallpaper* magazine). A few doors along is Cadenhead's Whisky Shop & Tasting Room, just the place for a wee dram to speed you on your way, while around 100m further on – on the left into Dorset Street – is an outpost of the superb

Nordic Bakery ⑮ , a delightful Scandinavian-style café serving food based on genuine Nordic recipes (don't miss the cinnamon buns!). Opposite is **The Barley Mow** ⑯ , a historic 18th-century pub with a vibrant atmosphere.

Just past the pub, turn right into Kendrick Place and walk to the top, then take another right into Paddington Street, where a short way along is leafy **Paddington Street Gardens** ⑰ . In summer you can hire a deckchair and enjoy a concert, while admiring the glorious trees, which include cherry, laburnum, hawthorn, London plane and a monkey puzzle, as well as shrubs, roses and seasonal bedding. Look out for the lovely statue of a young street cleaner, **Street Orderly Boy** ⑱ , by Milanese sculptor Donato Baraglia (1943). Some 30m after the gardens on the right is Grotto Passage, which recalls the Great Grotto where shell artist John Castles created, exhibited and sold his shell creations. It was a thriving business for 20 years from 1737 until Castles' death 20 years later. In 1846 the **Grotto Ragged and Industrial School** ⑲

Marylebone High Street

was established here, teaching destitute children practical skills.

Return to the entrance of Grotto Passage and cross over to go down Nottingham Place to Marylebone Road. Turn right past the Princess Grace Hospital to visit **St Marylebone Church** 🈠 (see box, below). This beautiful church is just as attractive inside, with a wealth of monuments, and its tranquil former churchyard stages the delightfully-named **Cabbages and Frocks** 🈠 market on Saturdays.

Almost opposite the church is the **Royal Academy of Music** 🈠, Britain's oldest degree-granting music school, founded in 1822. It's the UK's leading conservatoire and has trained thousands of accomplished musicians, including Sir Elton John, Annie Lennox, Michael Nyman and the late Sir Henry Wood (of Proms fame). Just past the academy turn right down Marylebone High Street, home to a plethora of tempting stores, boutiques, cafés, restaurants and pubs. Highlights include Michelin-starred Orrery at number 55, a superb French restaurant housed in a converted stable block, boasting a lovely rooftop terrace; **Daunt Books** 🈠 at numbers 83-84, occupying a beautiful Edwardian building dating from 1912 and believed to be the first custom-built bookshop in the world; Skandium at number 86, *the* place for clean Scandinavian design, from furniture and ceramics to fabric and toys; Anthropologie at number 33 (opposite) has iconic clothing, homeware and niche beauty products; the Marylebone on the corner of Moxon Street is an innovative pub and cocktail bar; and Kusmi Tea at number 15 is a wonderful tea emporium that's been trading since 1907. Marylebone Farmers' Market is held on Sundays (10am-2pm) in Cramer Street Car Park, just behind Waitrose.

Take a right down Blandford Street to admire the gothic glory of **St James's** 🈠 Roman Catholic church then return to Marylebone High Street and cross over to Marylebone Lane where, on the right-hand corner, is **Angel in the Fields** 🈠, one of the city's loveliest pubs. Shortly after the pub is the **Golden Hind** 🈠

St Marylebone Church

The present church, the fourth to serve the parish, was designed by Thomas Hardwicke and consecrated in 1817. Major alterations were made in 1885 – including new decorations in the Neoclassical style, combined with the pre-Raphaelite love of detail – which resulted in the magnificent church you see today (even though World War Two bombs blew out all the windows). The church has many historical links, including the secret marriage of poet Robert Browning and Elizabeth Barrett in 1846 after exchanging 574 love letters, which is commemorated by the Browning Chapel (1949). St Marylebone also has a well-deserved reputation for the excellence of its music, with concerts and recitals throughout the year.

St Christopher's Place

, an upmarket 'chippie' which has been providing superb fish suppers to the spoiled residents of Marylebone for over a century. Follow the lane round to the right to the **Coach Makers Arms** ㉗ , a refurbished gastropub from the Cubitt House hospitality group.

Around 50m after the junction with Hinde Street, take a right down Jason Court to Wigmore Street and cross over to **St Christopher's Place** ㉘ . This was once a slum, until social reformer Octavia Hill cleared it in the 1870s and named it in honour of St Christopher. Back then it was home to historic trades – from chandlers to cheese-mongers – but it's now a pedestrianised shopping and dining street, renowned for its diverse restaurants and cafés, with a cuisine to suit every palette. St Christopher's Place glides seamlessly into Gee's Court, which opens out onto Oxford Street; opposite is Bond Street tube station and the end of the walk.

Food & Drink

① **Landmark London:** Super venue for everything from a power breakfast to a candlelit dinner in the Winter Garden (hours vary, ££).

Natural Kitchen: Renowned café/restaurant and juice bar in Baker Street, serving fresh natural food (8am-10pm, weekends 9am-5pm, £).

⑮ **Nordic Bakery:** High-quality coffee, cakes and salads in a lovely relaxing space (7.30am-6.30pm, £).

㉗ **Coach Makers Arms:** Refurbished gastropub offering an all-day menu for breakfast, lunch and dinner (8am-11.30pm, £-££).

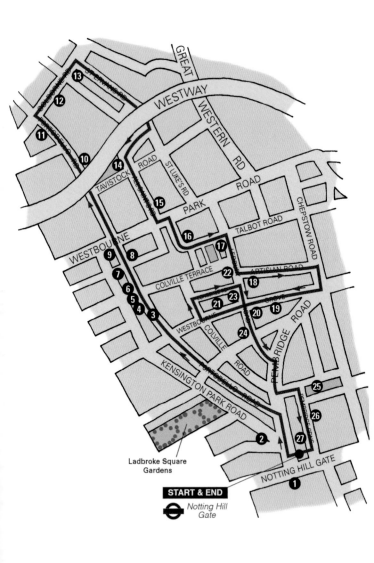

START & END

Notting Hill
Gate

WALK 16

● Places of Interest ● Food & Drink

Notting Hill

Walk 16

Distance: 3½ miles (5½ km)

Terrain: easy, a few hills

Duration: 2 hours

Start/End: Notting Hill Gate tube

Postcode/Parking: W11 3JS

NOTTING HILL

Once an inner-city slum, now a gentrified retreat with a bohemian edge, Notting Hill is one of the most cosmopolitan neighbourhoods in west London. Part of the Royal Borough of Kensington and Chelsea, it's best known for its annual Carnival and its colourful markets, such as the world-famous Portobello Road. It's also a socially diverse area: the southern squares and crescents around Notting Hill Gate are the preserve of the super-rich, while further up Ladbroke Grove, North Kensington has its fair share of social housing; this is where the Grenfell Tower fire tragedy occurred in July 2017.

The name Notting Hill first appears in records from 1356 as the charming Knottynghull, although the origin of the name is uncertain. Until the 18th century it was mainly farmland and gravel pits, but was developed in earnest from the early 19th century; it even had a racecourse in the late 1830s and some of its crescents follow the curves of the former course.

When building began in the 1830s, rows of smart terraces with hidden garden squares popped up alongside the shabby slums where brick makers and pig keepers lived – the so-called Potteries and Piggeries. In Victorian times most of Notting Hill was a rough working-class area, and by the '50s it had become synonymous with slum landlords and inner-city deprivation. Caribbean immigrants were drawn here by the affordable, if poor quality, housing – and this led to racial tensions that culminated in race riots in 1958.

In the '60s, Notting Hill began its renaissance, attracting media and creative types, which was further enhanced by the launch of the Notting Hill Carnival in 1965. By the '80s it was fast becoming one of London's most desirable places to live, and its image was further enhanced by the 1999 film, *Notting Hill*.

Today, Notting Hill has a reputation as an affluent and fashionable area, known for its attractive candy-coloured houses, antiques shops and market, superb restaurants, cool bars and characterful pubs. The walk takes in the length of Portobello Road, detouring via Golborne and Ledbury Roads, before returning to Notting Hill Gate.

Start Walking…

We start at Notting Hill Gate tube station – a toll gate stood here until 1864 – emerging on the north side of the street and taking the second right down Pembridge Road. Opposite is the ornate **Gate Cinema** ❶, which opened in 1911 as the Electric Palace, and a short way along Pembridge Road on the left is the **Gate Theatre** ❷, above the Prince Albert pub. Opened in 1979, the Gate is one of London's smallest off-West End theatres with just 75 seats, and has won numerous awards for its productions.

Take the second exit off the roundabout and continue north along Pembridge Road, turning left on Portobello Road by the Sun in Splendour pub. Probably Notting Hill's most famous street, thanks to the celebrated **Portobello Road Market** ❸ (see box, above), it's named after an English victory over Spain at Porto Bello in the

> ### Portobello Road Market
>
> London's largest and most popular market began in the 1860s when gypsies met here to trade in herbs and horses. Some 150 years later it's best known for its Saturday antiques market, although it's actually several markets rolled into one. These include Portobello Green Market (selling antiques, fashion, jewellery, cakes, food, books, etc., Fri-Sun) and Golborne Road Market (fruit and veg, street food, bric-a-brac, second-hand and household goods, Mon-Fri), in addition to the famous antiques market (the world's largest) on Saturdays, when over 1,000 dealers set up their stalls between Chepstow Villas and Elgin Crescent.

Gulf of Mexico in 1739. It begins as a quiet residential street with pastel-hued houses but once you cross Chepstow Villas, it becomes an antiques aficionado's Mecca with shops and arcades aplenty.

Portobello Road's other claim to fame is its cornucopia of trend-setting boutiques, cafés, restaurants and pubs. There are many popular places, but it's worth seeking out cocktail emporium **Trailer Happiness** ❹ (at number 177 on the corner of Elgin Crescent), which describes itself as a 'retro-sexy haven of

Portobello Road Market

cosmopolitan kitsch and faded trailer park glamour', and the **Electric Diner** ⑤ , a traditional diner offering a French-American menu in American-size portions (number 191). Next door to the diner is the **Electric Cinema** ⑥ , the city's first purpose-built cinema. It opened in 1910 and since then has been renamed ('30s), re-launched ('60s) and even had a notorious mass murderer (John Christie) working there ('40s). Now Grade II* listed, inside you're transported back to the '30s, with leather armchairs, footstools and side tables offering unparalleled comfort.

Electric Cinema

Just past the Electric Diner, take a detour down Blenheim Crescent on your left. Here you'll find the Spice Shop, the capital's best place to buy spices bar none, the **Notting Hill Bookshop** ⑦ – allegedly this is where Hugh Grant romanced Julia Roberts in *Notting Hill* – and, just over the road, Books for Cooks, London's best-smelling bookshop (recipes are tested daily in the café kitchen at the back). Returning to Portobello Road, turn left to pass **The Distillery** ⑧ at number 186 on the right, a working gin distillery offering masterclasses in London's famous spirit. Further up at number 225 is **The Castle** ⑨ pub, a popular people-watching spot.

Keep walking for around 300m, under the Westway flyover, and you come to **Acklam Village Market** ⑩ , a magnet for lovers of street food, serving snacks from Poland, Peru and Palestine (among other places). Almost next door at number 186 is another Portobello institution: Honest Jon's Records, a honey pot for vinyl fans since 1974. A few hundred metres further on, just before you turn right into Golborne Road, look for the **Spanish Institute** ⑪ (*Instituto Español*) on the left: a Spanish bilingual school housed in a lovely former Franciscan convent built in 1862. The school moved here in 1982, attracted by its Spanish connections; after the Spanish Civil War in the '30s, many political exiles and refugees settled locally.

Golborne Road, a buzzy, slightly scruffier version of Portobello Road, is packed with excellent eateries. At number 93 is **Snaps+Rye** ⑫ , a delightful Danish café-restaurant run by Jacqueline and Kell Skött,

Tabernacle

serving delicious food and coffee, while at number 57 is the **Lisboa Patisserie** ⓭, whose *pastéis de nata* (custard pies) are to die for. Just past the Lisboa turn right along St Ervans Road and follow the footpath at the end back under the Westway to Tavistock Crescent and turn right. Follow the road round to the right on All Saints Road, passing **Tavistock Gardens** ⓮ on your right; the next junction after Lancaster Road is **St Luke's Mews** ⓯, an attractive lane with some tragic history: in 2000, television presenter Paula Yates, ex-wife of singer and poverty campaigner Sir Bob Geldof, was found dead at number 4, aged just 41, the result of a heroin overdose. On a more cheerful note, the mews also featured in the film *Love Actually,* when Andrew Lincoln (Mark) declared his love for Keira Knightley (Juliet) using cue cards on the doorstep of number 27.

Continue to Westbourne Park Road, go left and then right into Powis Gardens and towards the end on the right is the church of All Saints Notting Hill, a Victorian Gothic Revival stone building dating from 1861. Carry on around to the left into Powis Square for

another interesting ecclesiastical building: the **Tabernacle** ⓰ is a striking 1887 building – originally an evangelical church – with an attractive curved Romanesque façade of red brick and terracotta, with towers with broach spires on both sides. Today, it's an arts, cultural and entertainment venue.

Carry on along the north side of Powis Square into Talbot Road, and turn right into Ledbury Road. On the corner is **The Ledbury** ⓱, a divine 2-star Michelin restaurant, rated one of

Notting Hill Carnival

Notting Hill hosts the largest street festival in Europe, where every August the streets are ablaze with extravagantly costumed dancers and decorated floats, and echo to the blare of calypso music and giant sound systems. Carnival takes place on the last Sunday and Monday of August and attracts well over a million revellers. Sunday is Children's Day, when the parade takes place over a shorter route and costume prizes are awarded, while Monday hosts the main cavalcade. The carnival began in 1965 as a small local affair, where west London's homesick Afro-Caribbean communities could celebrate their cultures and traditions, but has since become a major event on the capital's social calendar. It has its roots in the Caribbean carnivals of the mid-19th century – a particularly strong tradition in Trinidad – which celebrated the abolition of slavery.

the best in the world. Walk down Ledbury Road for 100m or so and turn left along Artesian Road, where after another 100m you come to the **Cock & Bottle** ⑱ , a refined Victorian free house with an upstairs dining room. At the end of the road turn right on Chepstow Road and right again into Westbourne Grove, another of Notting Hill's major thoroughfares. Around half way down on the

Granger & Co

left is **Granger & Co** ⑲ – one of three UK outlets from Australian celebrity chef Bill Granger – which does a bonzer breakfast/brunch.

Around 100m past Granger & Co on the right is **Westbourne Grove Church** ⑳ , a Gothic Baptist church built in 1823 and financed entirely by the congregation, mainly local shopkeepers and small businesses. From here, cross over Ledbury Road and around 50m up on the right opposite Lambton Place is the **202 Café** ㉑ , an elegant café secreted away in a Nicole Farhi boutique. During the week it's a peaceful spot to enjoy a morning coffee, though at weekends you're likely to have to queue for a table. Take the next right into Colville Road and right again into Lonsdale Road, which takes you back to Ledbury Road. A short way up on the left is a branch of the phenomenally successful **Matches** ㉒ , one of London's best designer fashion outlets – but you're turning right, passing a branch of **Ottolenghi** ㉓ , the upmarket deli chain founded by Israeli-born chef Yotam Ottolenghi. Its theme is imaginative Mediterranean-style dishes with a Middle Eastern influence. Continue south along Ledbury Road to pass

Food & Drink

⑤ **Electric Diner:** An American-style diner with a French influence on Portobello Road (8am-midnight, later at weekend, £).

⑫ **Snaps+Rye:** This cosy café on Golborne Road serves Danish specialities such as rye bread open sandwiches and much more (9am-5pm, 11pm Thu-Sat, closed Mon, £).

⑱ **Cock & Bottle:** A beautifully restored traditional pub, offering good ales, wines and food (noon-11/11.30pm, £).

⑲ **Granger & Co:** Aussie café/restaurant serving comfort food with a healthy twist (7am-11pm, £).

Beach Blanket Babylon 24, a Rococo-styled bar and vaulted modern European cellar restaurant in a Georgian townhouse.

Ledbury Road flows into Chepstow Crescent, at the end of which you turn right into Pembridge Villas. After around 100m go right again into **Pembridge Square 25**, with the Notting Hill Hotel on your right, and walk along the western edge of the square to turn right into Pembridge Gardens with its elegant Victorian townhouses. On the left is the HQ of **The Order of Women Freemasons 26** formed in 1908, a separate group from the 300-year-old United Grand Lodge of England, which doesn't allow women to enter its hallowed ranks. Some 200m further up on the right is the **Laslett 27**, a contemporary boutique hotel that takes its name from Rhaune Laslett, founder of the Notting Hill Carnival. The hotel lobby is a popular neighbourhood hangout, incorporating a lounge, library and designer boutique, and the Henderson bar and coffee shop serving breakfast, cocktails and an irresistible array of tasty dishes.

From the Laslett, it's a short stroll back down to Notting Hill Gate and its tube station – and the end of the walk.

Portobello Road

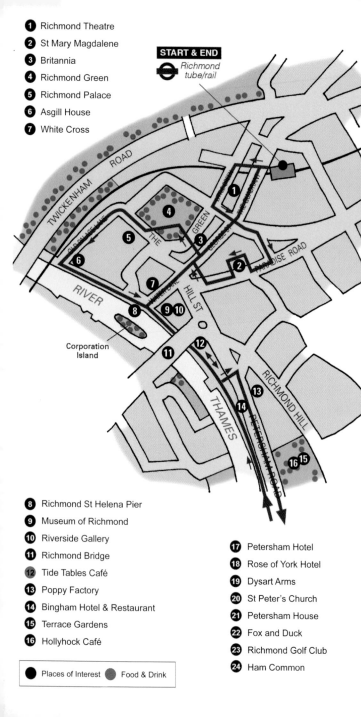

1 Richmond Theatre
2 St Mary Magdalene
3 Britannia
4 Richmond Green
5 Richmond Palace
6 Asgill House
7 White Cross

START & END
Richmond tube/rail

TWICKENHAM ROAD

OLD PALACE LANE

THE GREEN

GEORGE ST

PARADISE ROAD

RIVER

Corporation Island

HILL ST

THAMES

RICHMOND HILL

PETERSHAM ROAD

8 Richmond St Helena Pier
9 Museum of Richmond
10 Riverside Gallery
11 Richmond Bridge
12 Tide Tables Café
13 Poppy Factory
14 Bingham Hotel & Restaurant
15 Terrace Gardens
16 Hollyhock Café

17 Petersham Hotel
18 Rose of York Hotel
19 Dysart Arms
20 St Peter's Church
21 Petersham House
22 Fox and Duck
23 Richmond Golf Club
24 Ham Common

● Places of Interest ● Food & Drink

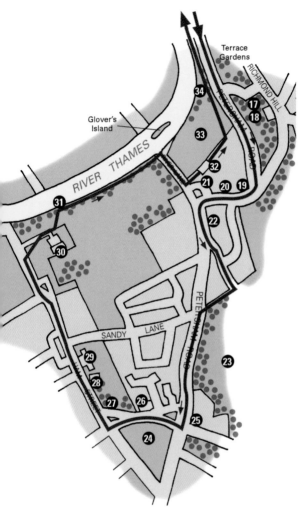

WALK 17

Richmond, Petersham & Ham

Distance: 6½ miles (10½ km)
Terrain: moderate, some steep hills
Duration: 3-4 hours
Start/End: Richmond tube/rail
Postcode: TW9 1DN

RICHMOND, PETERSHAM & HAM

Richmond-upon-Thames (to use its full title) is one of the jewels in southwest London's crown, best known for its ravishing riverside location, glorious deer park and links to British royalty. The satellite villages of Petersham and Ham – ancient settlements in their own right – are just as worthy of attention, and are included in this walk.

A London borough since 1965 – previously a town in Surrey – Richmond was originally known as Sheen, or Sceon (Saxon spelling). Its royal connections go back to the 14th century, when Edward I held court at Sheen Palace, and the King (or Queen) was Lord of the Manor; indeed, parts of Richmond are still owned by the Crown Estate. It was Henry VII, formerly the Earl of Richmond (in Yorkshire), who rebuilt the palace and named it after his ancestral home – and Richmond Palace was a favourite of British monarchs until the mid-17th century. The royal association led to the early growth of Richmond, which continued to develop as a fashionable town after it ceased to have a royal residence. Today, with its glorious Georgian townhouses, charming cottages, welcoming riverside pubs and stunning riverbank – not to mention excellent shopping, fine restaurants and lively theatres – Richmond is one of London's most desirable places to live.

The neighbouring villages of Petersham and Ham are tucked into a great sweeping curve on the south bank of the Thames. The earliest record of Petersham is in 666 as an endowment by Frithwald, Viceroy of Surrey, of all the chapels and lands held by the church at Kingston, to the Benedictine Abbey of St Peter in Chertsey. The village was recorded as Piterichesham (homestead of Patricius or Patrick) in the *Domesday Book* of 1086, while Ham isn't mentioned but may derive its name from the literal meaning of a meadowland in a river bend or *hamm*.

Richmond, Petersham & Ham

St Mary Magdalene

Petersham was described in the 18th century as the most elegant village in England and still has a unique charm. Unlike Richmond, the railways never reached Petersham or Ham, therefore they avoided the rapid expansion of the Victorian era. They have managed to hang on to their distinctive rural character into the 21st century, and are notable for their river meadows and commons, handsome houses and gentle pace of life.

Start Walking…

Leaving Richmond station, cross the main road and go down Old Station Passage (almost opposite) and turn left into Little Green (the road), which leads to Little Green (the park). Overlooking Little Green is the glorious **Richmond Theatre** ❶; built in red brick with buff terracotta and opened in 1899, it's one of the finest surviving examples of the work of leading theatre architect Frank Matcham. It's deservedly Grade II* listed and has a lovely interior. Take the next left to Duke Street and go straight across at the end to The Square and turn right down

Eton Street to Paradise Road. Just around the corner to the left is Hogarth House, former home of writer Virginia Woolf, but you turn right towards the river, passing pretty St James's Cottages some 50m along on the right and then, a little further on, the church of **St Mary Magdalene** ❷. Christians have worshipped on this site since the first chapel was built in around 1220. The church was entirely rebuilt in 1487-1506, although it has been much altered since.

Follow Church Walk anticlockwise around the church, past its main entrance, and back to Paradise Road. Turn right and take the next right along Victoria Place to George Street, where you cross the road and go right. Take the first left on Brewers Lane, where half way down on

Richmond Green

Richmond Palace

Now Grade I listed, the palace was built in 1501 by Henry VII, close to the site of Sheen Palace which had been built a few centuries earlier. It was a favourite home of Elizabeth I, who died there in 1603, and remained a residence of the kings and queens of England until the execution of Charles I in 1649, after which it was largely demolished. A few strikingly handsome buildings remain, including the Wardrobe, Trumpeters' House and the Gate House.

the right is the **Britannia** ❸ , the oldest pub in the borough, with a leafy garden and a modern British menu. Brewers Lane brings you out on to The Green opposite **Richmond Green** ❹ , where you take the diagonal path leading to the western perimeter. Richmond Green (12 acres/4.8ha) was described by architectural authority Nikolaus Pevsner as 'one of the most beautiful urban greens surviving anywhere in England'. Consisting of open grassland bordered by mature trees, it's been a venue for tournaments, archery and prize fights, and cricket matches have been played here since the 17th century. Turn right on to The Green and a short way along on the left is the

Wardrobe leading to Old Palace Yard and the site of the lovely weathered remains of **Richmond Palace** ❺ (see box, left).

Go past the Wardrobe and take the second left down Old Palace Lane to reach the Thames towpath. The house on the left-hand corner at the end is **Asgill House** ❻ , a Grade I listed Palladian villa dating from 1758; there's a plaque on the wall in Old Palace Lane commemorating the royal residents of Richmond Palace. Once on the towpath you have a good view of Richmond Railway Bridge and, just beyond that, Twickenham Bridge, before you turn left towards Richmond Bridge. The riverside path here is called Cholmondeley (pronounced Chumley) Walk and was reputedly the first public footpath in England – it's named after the Earl of Cholmondeley, an early resident.

After a few hundred metres you arrive at the **White Cross** ❼ , a Young's pub with a riverside terrace and a history going back to the 18th century, when it was called the Waterman's Arms; it's located just before Water Lane, where there's a slipway. Opposite the pub's terrace is **Richmond St Helena Pier** ❽ , where (in summer) you can board a boat

Richmond riverfront

Richmond, Petersham & Ham

to Hampton Court and Kingston, while beyond it is Corporation Island, an unpopulated, heavily wooded island. At certain times of the year the riverside path can flood, and in the 18th century there were two paths: a wet path for tradesmen and a dry path for gentle folk. Just past Water Lane, up some steps to Whittaker Avenue, are the **Museum of Richmond ⑨** and the **Riverside Gallery ⑩**, both located in the Old Town Hall (1893), and well worth a visit if you have a few hours to spare.

Continue along the towpath, past the grass terraces of Heron Square (see box, below) and boathouses, to **Richmond Bridge ⑪**, a handsome 18th-century (Grade I listed) stone arch bridge that's the oldest surviving Thames bridge in London. Under the arches is the **Tide Tables**

Richmond Bridge

Café **⑫**, a cool veggie/vegan café with a large, tree-shaded terrace. Follow the path under the bridge to Buccleuch Passage which is bordered by attractive gardens and mature trees. There are a number of pubs and restaurants fronting the river here, including the Gaucho restaurant in the shadow of a gigantic London Plane tree some 38m (125ft) tall. A short way after Gaucho take the path up through the garden to Petersham Road, where the **Poppy Factory ⑬** lies opposite; this is where Remembrance Day poppies are made – visits can be arranged (see www.poppyfactory. org/visit-us). Just past the factory on the right is the **Bingham Hotel & Restaurant ⑭**, which has a lovely terrace on the river.

As Petersham Road dips back towards the river, on your left are the beautiful **Terrace Gardens ⑮**, perched on a steep slope with spectacular views. The gardens contain many unusual trees, including redwood, maidenhair, spruce and cedars, along with a rose garden, flowerbeds and an herbaceous border. Near the entrance is the enchanting **Hollyhock Café ⑯** – a lovely place for morning coffee

---

Heron Square

Unlike many of the beautiful buildings in Richmond which date from the 1700-1800s, the handsome Heron Square development between Whittaker Avenue and Richmond Bridge is neo-Georgian, built in 1987 by Quinlan Terry (the giveaway is the lack of chimneys). Beyond the terraces, Heron Square hosts a Saturday Foodies Market (11am-4pm) and a Sunday Artisan Food & Craft Market (10.30am-5pm).

or afternoon tea. Continue along Petersham Road, passing Terrace Field and then Nightingale Lane, which leads to the celebrated **Petersham Hotel** ⑰ , with its award-winning restaurant, and on to Richmond Hill. Soon after Nightingale Lane you come to the **Rose of York Hotel** ⑱ – a Sam Smith's establishment with a large beer garden – and opposite there's a gate leading to Petersham Meadows. A few steps further along take the woodland path running along the edge of the meadows, which brings you out on the edge of Petersham village.

> ### St Peter's Church
>
> St Peter's is Grade II* listed and mostly dates from the 16th century, although parts of the chancel are 13th century, and it's believed there has been a church on the site since Saxon times. The well-preserved interior includes Georgian box pews, a two-deck pulpit (1796) and the royal arms of the House of Hanover from 1810. A number of notable people are buried in the churchyard, including naval Captain George Vancouver (1757-1798), best-known for his 1791-95 expedition which charted North America's Pacific Coast region, and after whom Vancouver Island and city are named.

Petersham Hotel

Turn right on Petersham Road and a short way along on the right is the **Dysart Arms** ⑲ , a superb restaurant located in an Arts and Crafts building dating from 1904 (booking essential, 020-8940 8005, closed Mon-Tue). It's named after the Earls of Dysart, who owned Ham House (see below) and the surrounding manors of Ham and Petersham for over 300 years. Just past the Dysart take a detour up Church Lane to see **St Peter's Church** ⑳ (see box).

There are many fine 17th and 18th-century mansions – Grade I or II* listed – in the immediate area formed by the junction of Petersham Road and River Lane (on the right). These include Rutland Lodge, built in 1666 for the Lord Mayor of London; Montrose House – adjacent to Rutland Lodge – the former home of entertainer Tommy Steele; Douglas House, where Catherine, Duchess of Queensberry was an 18th-century resident, now the home of the German School; and **Petersham House** ㉑ , dating from 1680 and now home to the Boglione family, owners of the acclaimed Petersham Nurseries. The house, which adjoins the nurseries, has a lovely garden that can be visited during the National Garden Scheme (www.ngs.org.uk).

From the church, continue along Petersham Road round the tight bend until, after around 100m, you reach Forge Lane, where there's a tiny white, weather-boarded 18th-century watchman's box and

Richmond, Petersham & Ham

village lock-up – used to detain drunks and other miscreants in bygone times. Opposite is Tree Close, once the driveway to Ham House, guarded by an imposing 'Jacobean' gatehouse built in 1900. It's also the entrance to Ham Polo Club and the German School. Just past Forge Lane is the **Fox and Duck** 🄰, a friendly sports pub which hosts live music on Saturday evenings.

A short way past the pub, bear left to Sudbrook Lane which has more fine old houses, although more modest than the grand mansions you passed earlier. In one of them, Elm Lodge (on the right opposite Bute Avenue), Charles Dickens wrote *Nicholas Nickleby* in summer 1839, which is commemorated by Dickens Close on the right. At the end of the lane is the entrance to Sudbrook Park, home of exclusive **Richmond Golf Club** 🄳, founded in 1891; Grade I listed Sudbrook House – designed by James Gibb and completed around 1728 – is now the clubhouse.

Ham Common

Turn right into Hazel Lane, a narrow walkway which leads back to Petersham Road where you go left. Continue south along Petersham Road for around 500m to **Ham Common** 🄴, which lost much of its land to the creation of Richmond Park in the 1600s, but still extends to 120 acres (49ha). The common is divided into distinct habitats – grassland and woodland – separated by Upper Ham Road, and is an area of ecological, historical and recreational interest. The grassland area has a cricket pitch in the middle and a pond in the northwest corner.

Food & Drink

🄬 **Tide Tables Café:** Hip veggie and vegan café in the converted arches of Richmond Bridge (8.30am-6.30/8pm, £).

🄿 **Ham Brewery Tap:** A friendly village pub in Ham, offering good ales and traditional pub grub (noon-midnight, £)

🄲 **Petersham Nurseries:** This renowned café is a delightful place for lunch (020-8332 8665, noon-5pm, closed Mon, ££), although booking is usually essential. There's also a pretty teahouse (9am-5pm, from 11am Sun, £).

On the corner of Ham Common, take a left down Ham Gate Avenue to **Ormeley Lodge** ㉕, an early 18th-century Georgian house owned by Lady Annabel Goldsmith, widow of tycoon Sir James Goldsmith; she was the inspiration for the London nightclub Annabel's which was founded by her first husband, Mark Birley. Return to Petersham Road and cross over to Ham Common (the road), which skirts the northern edge of the green. **St Michael's Convent** ㉖ can be spotted on the right. It was founded in 1870 by the Community of the Sisters of the Church, a religious order of around 100 women who live a vowed life of poverty, chastity and obedience.

Petersham Nurseries

At the western end of Ham Common turn right into Ham Street, the main village thoroughfare. St Thomas Aquinas Catholic Church is on the left, occupying a former 19th-century school, and almost immediately on the right is the **Ham Brewery Tap** ㉗, a friendly, traditional village pub. Much of Ham is now given over to modern estates, but a number of large period houses survive. Around 250m up on

the right are the **Algernon Tollemache Almshouses** ㉘, dating from 1892, and **Grey Court School** ㉙, which incorporates Newman House, the childhood country home of Cardinal John Henry Newman (1801-1890), marked with a blue plaque on the house itself – you can peek through the gates opposite Wiggins Lane. On the left is Ham's village green, which has a beautiful wildflower meadow in summer.

Continue along Ham Street, passing 18th-century Beaufort House on the right just past Sandy Lane; the former dower house to Ham House, it's now home to the Johnny Van Haeften gallery. Around 300m along on the right, just before Riverside Drive, is Melancholy Walk leading to Cut Throat Alley (the road-naming department must have been having a bad day!). At the end of Ham Street turn right past Ham House Stables, and a few hundred metres further on is **Ham House & Garden** ㉚ (see box, right), one of London's architectural and horticultural gems. The gardens are also home to the Orangery Café (10am-4pm).

Just past the garden bear left towards the river and **Hammertons Ferry** ㉛, which operates a year-round service for pedestrians and cyclists to Marble Hill Park on the north bank of the Thames (see www. hammertonsferry.com for the schedule). Turn right on to the Thames Path, passing the grounds of Ham Polo Club and Petersham Lodge Woods to

River Lane, where you turn right. After around 250m turn left along Church Lane past Petersham House to the outstanding **Petersham Nurseries** 32 . Not your usual garden centre, it's more famous for its delightful café/restaurant than its horticultural excellence. The café is a great place for lunch and there's also a pretty teahouse. A short way past the nurseries turn left along the footpath and cross **Petersham Meadows** 33 , part of the Ham House estate until the late 19th century and now preserved (as part of the view from Richmond Hill) for posterity, where you may see cows grazing. At the end of the meadows go left and enter **Buccleuch Gardens** 34 via a kissng gate on the right.

Exiting the gardens you're back on the Thames Path, which you follow north under Richmond Bridge. Go right on Water Lane by the White Cross pub and cross over to George Street, which takes you back to Richmond station – and the end of the walk.

Ham House & Garden

A National Trust property (free entrance for NT members), Ham House was built in 1610 for Sir Thomas Vavasour, Knight Marshal to James I, and was extended and refurbished as a palatial villa under the ownership of Lord and Lady Dysart (Elizabeth Maitland, Duchess of Lauderdale). The meticulously restored house has rooms of sumptuous splendour, decorated with tapestries, rich fabrics, rococo mirrors and spectacular collections of furniture, textiles and paintings, while the faithfully restored 17th-century formal garden (17 acres/7ha) is a remarkable survivor. For opening times, see www.nationaltrust.org.uk/ham-house-and-garden.

Petersham Meadows

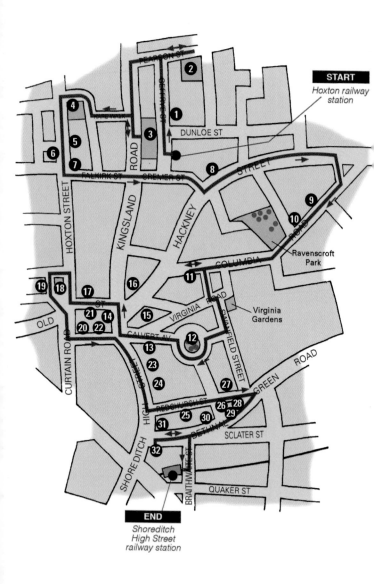

PEARSON ST

② 2

GEFFRYE ST

④ 4

HARE WALK

① 1

DUNLOE ST

③ 3

⑤ 5

ROAD

⑥ 6

⑦ 7

FALKIRK ST

CREMER ST

STREET

⑧ 8

⑨ 9

ROAD

KINGSLAND

HACKNEY

⑩ 10

Ravenscroft
Park

HOXTON STREET

COLUMBIA

⑯ 16

⑪ 11

⑲ 19

⑱ 18

⑰ 17

ST

Virginia
Road

Virginia
Gardens

OLD

CURTAIN ROAD

㉑ 21

⑭ 14

⑮ 15

VIRGINIA

CRANFIELD STREET

⑳ 20

㉒ 22

CALVERT AV.

⑫ 12

⑬ 13

㉓ 23

ROAD

HIGH STREET

㉔ 24

㉗ 27

GREEN

REDCHURCH ST.

㉖ 26 ㉘ 28

㉙ 29

㉛ 31

㉕ 25

㉚ 30

SHOREDITCH

BETHNAL

SCLATER ST

㉜ 32

BRAITHWAITE ST

QUAKER ST

● Places of Interest ● Food & Drink

WALK 18

Shoreditch & Hoxton

Distance: 3 miles (5 km)

Terrain: easy, largely flat

Duration: 1½ hours

Start: Hoxton rail

End: Shoreditch High St rail

Postcode: E2 8FF

SHOREDITCH & HOXTON

Now the haunt of London's hippest hipsters, Shoreditch and Hoxton have an intriguing history and offer a cornucopia of attractions – from music halls and markets to cocktail bars and cutting-edge designer stores. Now part of the East London borough of Hackney, they trace their origins back to the 12th century when Hoxton was a rural enclave, while Shoreditch was the site of Holywell Priory until 1539.

The name Shoreditch comes from Soersditch, which may derive from a small brook or sewer called the Soer (it could also be named after Sir John de Soerdich, Lord of the Manor during the reign of Edward III, 1327–77). Hoxton is first recorded in the *Domesday Book* as 'Hogesdon', meaning an Anglo-Saxon farm or fortified enclosure belonging to Hoch or Hocq. In medieval times, it formed a rural part of Shoreditch parish and achieved independent ecclesiastical status in 1826, although civil jurisdiction remained with Shoreditch vestry.

By the late Middle Ages Shoreditch had become rather sleazy, which made it an apt location for London's earliest theatre in 1576, as it was just outside the jurisdiction of the City of London. In the 17th century its fortunes improved, when Huguenot silk weavers established a textile industry; by this time neighbouring Hoxton had become fashionable, with many large houses, squares and almshouses. However, both areas declined from the late 18th century when they were overwhelmed by industrial development, and by the end of the 19th century both areas (particularly Shoreditch) were home to swathes of Dickensian slum housing. They suffered badly from the advent of the railways, and vast tracts were later destroyed during the Blitz.

Shoreditch & Hoxton

Gentrification began in the '90s with the dot.com boom (many web-based businesses located here) and today, Shoreditch and Hoxton are a magnet for creative types – and a grand canvas for graffiti artists. The former Victorian factories and warehouses have been converted into luxury apartments, galleries, designer hotels and shops, cool eateries, bars and clubs. More than anywhere else, Shoreditch and Hoxton are emblematic of the East End's phoenix-like rise from post-industrial wasteland to become a place of relentless re-invention and innovation – and, as such, they're an enthralling area to explore.

Start Walking...

From Hoxton railway station head right along Geffrye Street, where tucked under a railway arch is the **Fabrique Bakery** ❶ , serving tasty coffee and cinnamon buns. Around 50m past the bakery turn right on Pearson Street to discover the award-winning **St Mary's Secret Garden** ❷ (Mon-Fri, 9am-5pm) a lovely hidden oasis named for St Mary, Haggerston, which was built nearby by John Nash in 1827, but destroyed in World War Two. Leaving the garden, turn left on Pearson Street to Kingsland Road, where you go left to see the **Geffrye Museum** ❸ (see box). From the Geffrye, retrace your steps a little way and go left down Hare Walk and then right at the end on Stanway Street, which leads round to Hoxton Street. The main thoroughfare of Hoxton,

Geffrye Museum

This enchanting collection traces the changing style of domestic interiors from 1600 to the late 20th century. It's located in a row of almshouses, which were built in 1714 by the Ironmongers' Company with a bequest from Sir Robert Geffrye, twice master of the company and a former Lord Mayor of London. Unfortunately the museum closed for redevelopment in January 2018 (see www.geffrye-museum.org.uk for information) but keep it in mind for future exploration when it reopens in 2020.

Hoxton Street retains some of its former village character and hosts a lively market (Mon-Fri 11am-3pm, Sat 9am-4pm). Established in 1687, Hoxton Street Market is the oldest street market in Hackney.

Turn left to pass the award-winning **Hoxton Trust Community Garden** ❹ , created in the early '80s to build the skills, knowledge and confidence of the community. Its site was the location of an 18th-century lunatic

Hoxton Hall

In 1605, Guy Fawkes's plot to blow up the Houses of Parliament was exposed in a letter delivered to a house in Hoxton Street. A plaque to this effect is attached to the end wall of a building on the west side of Hoxton Street just after the junction with Crondall Street.

asylum, Holly House, and contains the 19th-century cupola and clock from the old Eastern Fever Hospital at nearby Homerton. A little further along is Grade II* listed **Hoxton Hall** ❺, an East End landmark built as a music hall in 1863. It was restored to its former glory in 2015 – a two-tier galleried auditorium rising on three sides, supported on cast-iron columns with iron railings – and is now a community centre and performance space. Cross the street to what's possibly London's wackiest shop, **Hoxton Street Monster Supplies** ❻, which styles itself 'London's oldest supplier of goods for the living, dead and undead'!

Around 50m further on, take a left down Falkirk Street, just past **The Bach Hoxton** ❼, a scrumptious Kiwi café serving super coffee with an innovative breakfast/brunch menu containing vegetarian and vegan dishes. Continue along Falkirk Street,

passing Hackney College on the right, and cross over Kingsland Road where there's a plethora of inexpensive (and delicious) Vietnamese restaurants, cafés and shops – not for nothing is it dubbed the 'Pho Mile'. Carry on to Cremer Street and turn left at the end along Hackney Road, passing another superb Kiwi licensed café/gallery on the left, **Long White Cloud** ❽, serving excellent coffee and creative food. A bit further up, after Weymouth Terrace, is Morito from Sam & Sam Clark, serving inventive tapas dishes from Spain and North Africa.

Columbia Road Flower Market

London's most colourful street market on Sundays – and the city's only dedicated flower market – Columbia Road grew from the seeds of a 19th-century food market surrounded by Victorian shops. The area went into decline in the '70s, and the historic street faced demolition, but a local campaign saved it and the market blossomed again in the '80s. On Sundays Columbia Road is transformed into a sea of foliage and flowers, everything from bedding plants to 10-foot banana trees, many of which are available at knock-down prices.

Around 200m past Morito, cross the road and turn down Ropley Street and then right to Columbia

Road, which hosts the famous **Columbia Road Flower Market**  ❾ (see box opposite). It's worth a visit on any day as it's home to some 60 independent shops, plus a wealth of outstanding pubs, cafés and restaurants, including the Royal Oak, a pub of two halves, with a boisterous downstairs bar and a more sedate dining room upstairs.

Arnold Circus

Arnold Circus is the centrepiece of the redbrick Boundary Estate, the world's first council estate and one of the most architecturally unique; it was formally opened in 1900 and replaced the Old Nichol Street Rookery, one of the East End's most notorious slums. The estate consists of multi-storey tenements radiating from the central circus, each bearing the name of a location along the Thames. Soil from the foundations was used to construct a mound in the middle of the Circus, surmounted by a bandstand.

Continue along Columbia Road, passing the outstanding **Brawn** ❿ restaurant on the corner of Ravenscroft Street – opposite The Birdcage, a restored Victorian gastropub – and go straight across at the roundabout. Around 150m up on the left, just past Gascoigne Place, is the Grade II listed **Leopold Buildings** ⓫ , a historic tenement block of flats built in 1872 by the Improved Industrial Dwellings Company, founded and chaired by Sir Sydney Waterlow. It was built on land leased by Angela Burdett-Coutts, then the richest woman in Britain; noted for her philanthropy, she was nicknamed

the 'Queen of the Poor'. Turn down Gascoigne Place, cross over and take Swanfield Street (past Virginia Gardens) and turn right into Palissy Street. At the end of the street is **Arnold Circus** ⓬ (see box, below).

Walk around the Circus in a clockwise direction – passing the superb Rochelle Canteen, a local destination restaurant in a converted bike shed – and take the fifth exit to Calvert Avenue, home to a wealth of interesting shops. These include delightful Leila's Shop on the right (old-fashioned grocer meets modern café), Ally Capellino (elegant bags) and Luna & Curious (exquisite lifestyle boutique). At number 22 is the **Calvert 22 Foundation** ⓭ , a non-profit gallery specialising in Eastern European contemporary art and culture. At the end of the avenue turn right on Shoreditch High Street, the main thoroughfare of Shoreditch, where opposite is the award-winning flagship store of the celebrated **House of Hackney** ⓮ , a temple of modern interior design. Next door is the decorative façade of the former Wells & Co foundry and showroom, now shops and a bar.

St Leonard's, Shoreditch

A little way along on the right, on the corner of Hackney Road, is **St Leonard's, Shoreditch** ⑮ . Dedicated to the patron saint of prisoners and the mentally ill, among others, it's a starkly beautiful church dating from around 1740, designed by George Dance the Elder, a pupil of Sir

Shoreditch Town Hall

Dating from 1866, this was one of the grandest vestry halls (council chamber) of its time and played an important role in East End working-class culture, first as an assembly and music hall in the late 19th and early 20th centuries, and later as a boxing venue from 1955 to 1975. It fell into disrepair in the '80s, but was saved in 2002 and is now a flagship arts, events and community space.

Food & Drink

- ① **Fabrique Bakery:** Start the day well at this Swedish bakery/café (Mon-Fri 8am-6pm, Sat-Sun 9am-6pm, £)

- ⑧ **Long White Cloud:** Ethically-sourced breakfast, brunch and coffee in a simple, white-box café hosting regular art shows (7/8am-5pm, £).

- ⑩ **Brawn:** Celebrated European-style cuisine with a daily changing menu of seasonal produce served in two simple but stylish rooms (020-729 5692, Tue-Sun noon-3pm, Mon-Sat 6-10.30/11pm, £-££).

- ㉓ **Dishoom:** A wonderfully kitsch café-restaurant serving Raj-style treats, from Bombay breakfast to afternoon *chai* (8/9am-11pm/midnight, £).

Christopher Wren. The church is mentioned in the nursery rhyme *Oranges and Lemons* in the line '*When I grow rich, say the bells of Shoredith*'. It's the resting place of many prominent Tudor actors, including James Burbage who founded England's first successful playhouse, The Theatre, in Shoreditch in 1576, and his son Richard, a leading player in many of Shakespeare's plays. In front of the church is the Clerk's House – at number 118½ Shoreditch High Street (in earlier times letters weren't added to addresses as they are today) – which was originally occupied by clerics but now contains a shop. Opposite the church on Hackney ⑯ Road is **Perseverance Works** , a unique company owned by its shareholders and tenants – a community of around 600 who live and work in this vast creative hub.

Shoreditch & Hoxton

Just past the church, turn left into Old Street and look for the imposing **Shoreditch Town Hall** **17** (see box opposite) on the left after the bridge. Almost opposite the town hall is the Old Street Magistrate's Court and police station, now a luxury 5-star boutique hotel, where the notorious Kray twins were former 'guests' (in the police station lockup, not the hotel).

Around 50m past the town hall turn right on Hoxton Street and left into **Hoxton Square** **18** . Laid out in 1683, it's one of London's oldest garden squares; sadly, only a few of the original Georgian buildings remain – a good example is number 32. One of Hoxton Square's 18th-century residents was the Reverend John Newton, composer of *Amazing Grace*; another was Dr James Parkinson who discovered Parkinson's disease and has a blue plaque outside number 1 in the southwest corner of the square. Originally an industrial

hub, today the square is at the heart of Hoxton's arts and media scene, with many entertainment options. These include the Hoxton Square Bar & Kitchen, an arty restaurant and bar with live music and DJs, and **Happiness Forgets** **19** , a celebrated basement cocktail bar with a hint of the speakeasy about it.

32 Hoxton Square

From Hoxton Square, take Rufus Street south, crossing Old Street to Charlotte Road, and go left down Rivington Street – the heart of Shoreditch's buzzing nightlife. Cross Curtain Road to carry on along Rivington Street and as the cobbled street narrows, so the entertainment options broaden. On the left at number 65 is **Callooh Callay** **20** , an eccentric cocktail and party bar; loosely Lewis-Carroll-themed and named after an expression in his nonsense poem *Jabberwocky*, it's one of Shoreditch's most popular nightspots. Just up Rivington Place on the left is **Rivington Place Gallery** **21** , a public art gallery space dedicated to cultural diversity in the visual arts, housed in a RIBA award-winning building

---

Dishoom

Wonderfully kitsch, Dishoom is a modern take on the old Irani (Persian) style cafés that were popular in '60s Bombay (Mumbai). Its menu includes Bombay classics such as *pau bhaji* and *roomali roti*, while the faded retro design incorporates ceiling fans, bamboo blinds, cane furniture, vintage advertising and droll slogans ('All chai is coming strictly without opium'), along with a lovely Raj-style 'verandah'.

---

by David Adjays. A little further along is **Cargo** 22 , nestled under disused railway arches, a trailblazing nightclub, bar and restaurant with a large courtyard.

At the end of Rivington Street you're back on Shoreditch High Street, where former industrial buildings, warehouses and workshops have evolved into modern offices and hotels, and yet more hip bars, cafés and restaurants. Turn right and around 100m down on the left is the **Ace Hotel London** 23 (formerly the Shoreditch Empire theatre), one of Shoreditch's trendiest hangouts. Comfortable, stylish and slightly bohemian, its public spaces include a bar and art gallery, coffee shop, brasserie, and a basement bar with live music and DJs. A little further along is **Dishoom** 24 , (see box, page 165) one of the city's most innovative restaurants.

Just past Dishoom turn left into Redchurch Street, another of Shoreditch's gentrified thoroughfares, reborn as a place for upscale shopping, including fashion, galleries, interiors, beauty and foodie stores. On the left, on the corner of Boundary Street, is Sir Terence Conran's award-winning Boundary 'Project',

occupying a beautiful converted Victorian warehouse, comprising a boutique hotel, restaurants, bars, café, bakery and a delicatessen. Just past the Boundary on the right at number 34 is the delightfully named the **Owl & Pussycat** 25 , a traditional East End pub that has had a gastro makeover but retains its pubby atmosphere. A bit further down on the same side is Allpress Espresso, a popular (Kiwi-owned) artisan roastery café serving great coffee and tasty food. Just past Allpress in Club Row is the **Electric Cinema** 26 , a luxury, single-screen cinema with a bar and velvet furniture, showing mainstream and indie films.

Labour and Wait

Cross Club Row to continue along Redchurch Street and on the corner of Turville Street you'll find **Labour and Wait** 27 . Housed in an old Truman Brewery pub, this design store specialises in household goods: not your usual tat, but functional, well-designed, honest, timeless, aesthetically pleasing products to enhance everyday life.

At the end of the street turn sharp right into Bethnal Green Road, where on the right is

Dishoom

Brewdog Shoreditch 🟠, an outpost of the Aberdeenshire pub-brewery group Brewdog. Looking a bit like a metal-bashing factory, it's a place for real beer aficionados, serving a constantly changing selection of innovative craft beer and tasty food. Just past Brewdog is **Rich Mix** 🟠, a creative community arts hub staging music, dance, comics and spoken word performances, art shows and film screenings. Around 150m further along, just past Club Row, is **Beach Blanket Babylon** 🟠, an offshoot of the original cocktail bar in Notting Hill. This venue is a bar-cum-gallery with décor that's a blend of boho chic and French country château, with gilded wallpaper, over-the-top furniture and glitzy ornaments. The cocktail lounge can accommodate 300, while the restaurant seats 150, and there's also an enormous gallery space for exhibitions and special events.

Keep walking and on the corner of Ebor Street is **Shoreditch House** 🟠, a private members' club that's also a hotel which lets rooms to non-members. Occupying a converted warehouse, the hotel has a restaurant, spa, rooftop pool and gym. Over Bethnal Green Road is **Boxpark Shoreditch** 🟠, which combines the concepts of a modern street food market and a pop-up retail mall, created out of shipping containers (hence the name), specialising in fashion, arts, food and drinks. From here, retrace your steps along Bethnal Green Road and go right down Braithwaite Street to Shoreditch High Street station – and the end of the walk.

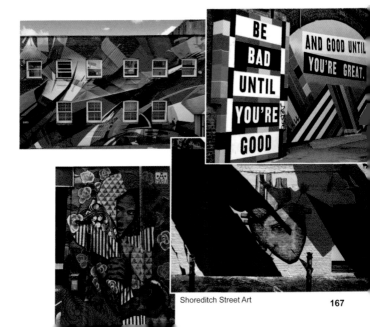

Shoreditch Street Art

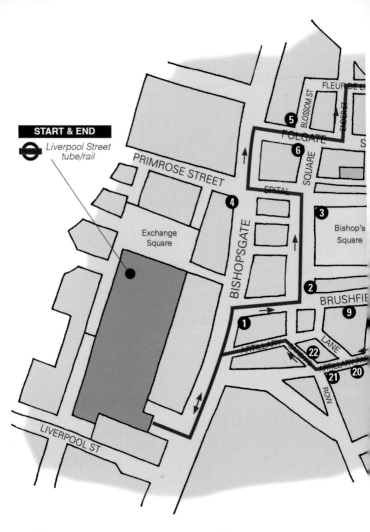

START & END

Liverpool Street tube/rail

FLEUR DE LI

BLOSSOM ST

PRIMROSE STREET

FOLGATE

⑤ Water Poet

⑥ Dennis Severs' House

SPITAL

SQUARE

④ Department of Coffee & Social Affairs

BISHOPSGATE

Exchange Square

③ Spitalfields Charnel House

Bishop's Square

② Goat Statue

BRUSHFIE

⑨ A. Gold

① Bishopsgate Institute

LANE

ARTILLERY

㉒

LIVERPOOL ST

ARTILLERY PAS

㉑ ⑳

ROW

---

① Bishopsgate Institute

② Goat Statue

③ Spitalfields Charnel House

④ Department of Coffee & Social Affairs

⑤ Water Poet

⑥ Dennis Severs' House

⑦ Hawksmoor

⑧ ● Old Spitalfields Market

⑨ A. Gold

⑩ Ten Bells

⑪ Christ Church Spitalfields

⑫ Jamme Masjid Mosque

● Places of Interest ● Food & Drink

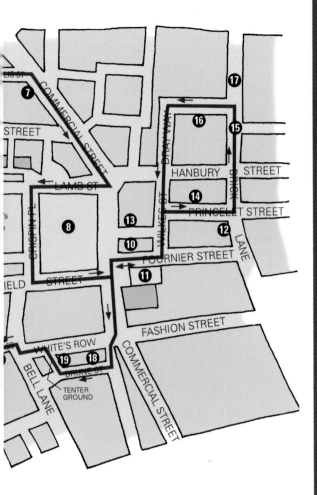

13 Norton Folgate Almshouses

14 Museum of Immigration & Diversity

15 Brick Lane

16 Old Truman Brewery

17 Brick Lane Market

18 Soup Kitchen for the Jewish Poor

19 Tenter Ground

20 56 & 58 Artillery Lane

21 Grapeshots

22 Sandys Row Synagogue

Spitalfields

Walk 19

Distance: 2 miles (3¼ km)
Terrain: easy, flat terrain
Duration: 1 hour
Start/End: Liverpool St tube/rail
Postcode: EC2M 7QH

SPITALFIELDS

Perched between the City and the East End of London, in the borough of Tower Hamlets, Spitalfields is a neighbourhood that's been moulded by migrants seeking sanctuary and a new life since the 17th century, from Protestant Huguenots and Irish weavers to Jewish refugees and Bengali entrepreneurs. As such it has a unique diversity and an enduring sense of community that sets it apart from other East End quarters.

The name Spitalfields is derived from St Mary Spital, a priory and hospital – one of the largest in medieval England – that was founded here in 1197. The area consisted largely of fields and nursery gardens until the 17th century when, after the destruction wrought by the Great Fire in 1666, Spitalfields was rebuilt as a planned suburb, one of the first in London.

The first Protestant Huguenots arrived in 1685, fleeing religious persecution in France, and bringing their skills in the silk industry; Irish weavers followed in the 1730s, attracted by opportunities in the silk trade. In the Victorian era, silk production declined and Spitalfields began attracting 'blue-collar' industries such as brewing, tanning, foundries and furniture making. However, by the 19th century there were acute problems with overcrowding, slums and prostitution, and it became one of London's most deprived districts, rife with crime. Nevertheless, it continued to attract newcomers: Irish workers escaping the potato famine and Jews driven out of Eastern Europe by the pogroms, and in the mid- to late-20th century, Bangladeshis, Bengalis and Somalis.

Since the '60s, Spitalfields' star has been in the ascendant. The subject of intensive regeneration and conservation, it's one of the capital's most exciting areas, full of boho chic. Its quaint cobbled streets and glorious Georgian houses are squeezed between the skyscrapers of Bishopsgate and the down-to-earth atmosphere of Brick Lane, with its all-night bagel shops, curry houses and markets. It may lack rose-covered cottages and a green, but Spitalfields remains very much a village at heart.

Start Walking…

Leave Liverpool Street station via the exit onto Bishopsgate, once the site of one of the original Roman city gates. Cross the road, turn left and a short way along is the **Bishopsgate Institute** , a celebrated cultural society established in 1895, housed in a striking Arts and Crafts building designed by Charles Harrison Townsend. Just past the Institute, turn right into Brushfield Street – stop to admire the view of Christ Church Spitalfields (see box, page 173) framed by the end of the street – and then go left to modern Bishops Square, passing the award-winning **Goat Statue** ❷, standing 11.5ft (3.5m) tall atop a stack of boxes, by Scottish sculptor Kenny Hunter. A little

further on is **Spitalfields Charnel House** ❸, a 14th-century crypt where human bones were stored. The site – preserved beneath glass – was once part of the cemetery of St Mary Spital Priory, which stood nearby.

Dennis Severs' House

One of London's most singular attractions in one of its most magical properties, Dennis Severs' House is part exhibition, part installation: a work of fantasy which creates an atmosphere redolent of the 18th century and paints a picture of what life was like then. It's the brainchild of American artist, Dennis Severs (1948-1999), who invented the Jervis family of Huguenot silk weavers, whose imagined lives became a detailed 'still life drama' for visitors. Each of the ten rooms reflects a different era of the building's past – a snapshot of the life of the family who 'lived' here between 1724 (when 18 Folgate Street was built) and 1914. The house is open for tours (fee) on selected days (see www.dennissevershouse.co.uk).

At the end of Bishops Square, turn left on Spital Square and right on Bishopsgate, then up to the junction with Folgate Street where, just opposite, is a branch of the **Department of Coffee & Social Affairs** ❹ – a good place for a caffeine fix. Cross back and walk down Folgate Street, home to some of Spitalfields'

Dennis Severs' House

Walk 19

best-preserved Georgian houses. On the corner of Blossom Street is the **Water Poet** (5), a gem of a gastropub, with creative food, fine ales and a huge beer garden. Just past the pub, on the right, is **Dennis Severs' House** (6) (see box, page 171), an 18th-century house-turned-museum.

Around 50m past Dennis Severs' House, turn left down Elder Street to admire more well-preserved 18th-century Huguenot architecture – number 32 on

the left was the home of painter Mark Gertler (indicated by a blue plaque), who was born in nearby Gun Street. Turn right on Fleur De Lis Street towards Commercial Street, one of Spitalfields' main thoroughfares, and the location of the first Peabody social housing estate, which opened in 1864, replacing some of London's worst slums. The building remains, but is now a private residential block. Turn right along Commercial Street, passing a branch of the excellent **Hawksmoor** (7) restaurant chain, a steakhouse and bar which also does an amazing breakfast.

A few hundred metres further on, turn right down Lamb Street to visit **Old Spitalfields Market** (8). Located in one of London's finest surviving Victorian market halls, dating from 1887, there's been a market here since 1638, when Charles I granted a licence for 'flesh, fowl and roots' to be sold on 'Spittle Fields'. The market buildings, hall and roof have been restored – resplendent under a Fosters + Partners glass canopy – offering a fusion of Victorian splendour and cutting-edge contemporary architecture. The market specialises in fashion, food, vintage and general goods, and has a wealth of eateries.

From Lamb Street head down Crispin Place through the market to return to Brushfield Street. Turn right and on the corner of Gun Street is the charming former (19th-century) store of Verde & Company at number 40, a foodie mecca that was forced to close in 2017 due to a sharp hike in

A. Gold

Located in a four-storey, Grade II listed building dating from 1780, A. Gold is currently home to Cundall & Garcia which styles itself as 'a village shop in the City' and is the only deli in London offering entirely British produce. The shop's original name refers to Amelie Gold, a Hungarian Jew who ran a French millinery shop here in the 1880s. Over the years it has housed a number of local businesses, from diamond cutters and furriers to drapers and bookbinders – but the original shop sign remains.

Christ Church Spitalfields

Designed by Nicholas Hawksmoor (1661-1736), the lovely 18th-century Christ Church Spitalfields (Mon-Fri 10am-4pm, Sun 1-4pm) is his Baroque masterpiece. It was built between 1714 and 1729 and is noted for the beauty of its stonework and pleasing geometry. Its architectural composition demonstrates Hawksmoor's usual abruptness: the plain rectangular box of the nave is surmounted at its west end by a broad tower of three stages, topped by a steeple that's more Gothic than classical (the magnificent porch was a later addition). Just as Christ Church is the masterpiece of its architect so the organ installed in 1735 was the tour de force of England's greatest organ builder, Richard Bridge.

business rates (from £21,500 to £54,000!), while next door – still hanging on – is old-fashioned grocer **A. Gold** ❾ (see box, left).

Head east up Brushfield Street and cross Commercial Street to Fournier Street where, on the corner, is the **Ten Bells** ❿ . This infamous hostelry dates back to 1755 and has associations with Jack the Ripper. At least two of his victims, Mary Kelly and Annie Chapman, drank or solicited business here, and Chapman is said to have been in the pub the night before her mutilated body was discovered in nearby Hanbury Street in November 1888. The pub's grim past has apparently left its mark, and a number of ghosts

are said to haunt it. Opposite the pub is **Christ Church Spitalfields** ⓫ (see box, left), one of London's most splendid churches.

Continue along Fournier Street, once the heart of Huguenot Spitalfields; the early 18th-century houses were originally built for silk weavers and have large latticed windows illuminating the top floor rooms that once housed the looms. At the end of the street (on the left) is the **Jamme Masjid Mosque** ⓬ , aka the Brick Lane Mosque. Built in 1743 as a Huguenot chapel, it has also served as a Methodist chapel and a Jewish synagogue, thus it's the only place of worship in London to have housed all three monotheistic traditions.

Retrace your steps to turn right along Wilkes Street, and take a detour down Puma Court on the left to see the **Norton Folgate Almshouses** ⓭ dating from 1860. Return to Wilkes Street and turn right into pretty Princelet Street, where at number 19 is the **Museum of Immigration & Diversity** ⓮ , Europe's only cultural institution devoted to the movement of people in search of a better life. It's housed in an unrestored (Grade II* listed) house built in 1719, which is so fragile that the museum is only open a few days a year. It was once home

Museum of Immigration & Diversity

Food & Drink

④ **Department of Coffee & Social Affairs:** Admirable coffee shop on Norton Folgate for an early/mid-morning caffeine shot (Mon-Fri 7am-5pm), £.

⑤ **Water Poet:** Boho pub just across from Dennis Severs' House serving gastro grub, with a reputation for an exceptional Sunday lunch, (11am/midday-11pm, £).

⑧ **Old Spitalfields Market:** From Climpson's coffee to the Duck Truck and Wright Brothers seafood, there's a wide choice of eateries in this trendy market place (Mon-Fri 10am-8pm, Sat-Sun 10am-5/6pm, £-££).

㉑ **Grapeshots:** Wine bar in Artillery Lane serving breakfast, lunch and dinner (Mon-Fri 10am-11pm, Sat 4-11pm, closed Sun, £).

Bricks and tiles were fired here in the 16th century, although it's now better known for its shopping and eating attractions. One of London's most colourful and multicultural streets, Brick Lane may be the best place in London for a curry, but if you fancy something different, number 159 is home to Brick Lane Beigel Bake, open 24 hours and reputedly London's oldest and best baker of beigels (or bagels). Turn left and walk north to the **Old Truman Brewery** ⑯ buildings (1666-1989), now home to an arts and media quarter, along with independent shops, galleries, bars and restaurants. Centred in and around the brewery are a number of markets, including **Brick Lane Market** ⑰ (see box, right).

56 Artillery Lane

From the markets, take Dray Walk south and cross Hanbury Street to Wilkes Street, which leads to Fournier Street. Turn right to return to Commercial Street, turn left and take the second right on White's Row; immediately bear left into Toynbee Street and then right to Brune Street. Halfway down on the right is the attractive **Soup Kitchen for the Jewish Poor** ⑱ , which dates back to 1902. This was a charity funded

to a Huguenot silk merchant, Peter Abraham Ogier, whose daughter Louisa Perina Courtauld (1729-1807), was the mother of George Courtauld, founder of the Courtaulds company in 1794.

At the end of Princelet Street, turn left into **Brick Lane** ⑮ .

Brick Lane Market

Although an entity in itself, Brick Lane Market is also a general term for a number of markets. These include the Backyard Market for arts and crafts, the Boiler House food market and the Brick Lane Tearooms, all open on Saturdays (11am-6pm) and Sundays (10am-5pm), plus the Vintage Market (Thu-Sat 11am-6pm, Sun 10am-6pm) and the Sunday Upmarket (10am-5pm) in Ely's Yard, the biggest draw by far. (For information see www.bricklanemarket.com.)

by wealthy Jews and although (ironically) it now houses luxury apartments, the fine façade has been preserved and you can still see the original 'Way In' and 'Way Out' signs above the doors. At the end of the street turn right on **Tenter Ground** ⑲ , where there are more attractive Huguenot buildings; it gets its name from the tenters (wooden frames) on which woven cloth was stretched to help it dry.

Turn left at the end of Tenter Ground, then right on Bell Lane and left into Artillery Lane. Take a moment to admire the 18th-century elegance of **56 & 58 Artillery Lane** ⑳ on the left. Both are Grade I listed, with bow windows and ornate carving, and date from 1705, although the magnificent Georgian shop front of number 56 is slightly newer (1756-7). Continue straight ahead into narrow Artillery Passage and look for **Grapeshots** ㉑ on the left (numbers 2/3), a characterful bar and dining room, owned by the Davy's Wine Bars chain.

At the end of the passage, turn right into Sandys Row, where a short way along is Grade II listed **Sandys Row Synagogue** ㉒ . Founded in 1854, it's the oldest Ashkenazi synagogue in London, although the building was built around 1766 as a Huguenot chapel. Sandys Row is one of only a handful of synagogues remaining in the East End, where there were once over 100. At the end of Sandys Row, turn left on Artillery Lane and walk to the end, crossing Bishopsgate to reach Liverpool Street station and the end of the walk.

Brick Lane Market

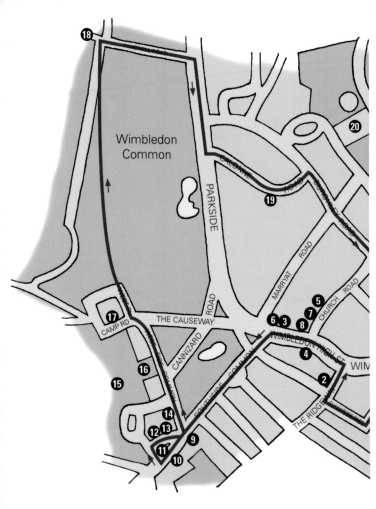

1. Kaldi Coffee
2. Museum of Wimbledon
3. Eagle House
4. Dog & Fox
5. Fire Stables
6. Rose & Crown
7. Old Fire Station
8. Maison St Cassien

9. King's College School
10. Southside House
11. Gothic Lodge
12. Crooked Billet
13. Hand in Hand
14. Chester House
15. Cannizaro Park
16. Hotel du Vin & Bistro Wimbledon

● Places of Interest   ● Food & Drink

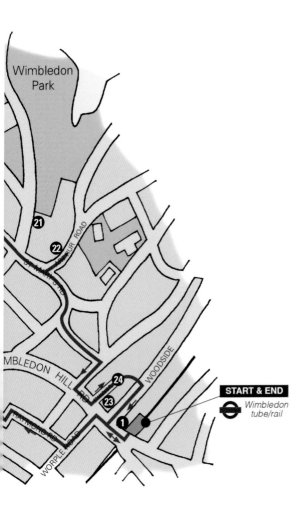

- **17** Fox & Grapes
- **18** Wimbledon Windmill Museum
- **19** Buddhapadipa Temple
- **20** All England Lawn Tennis and Croquet Club
- **21** Old Rectory
- **22** St Mary's Church
- **23** The Loft
- **24** St Mark's Church

Wimbledon

Distance: 5 miles (8 km)

Terrain: moderate, some hills

Duration: 2½ hours

Start/End: Wimbledon tube/rail

Postcode/Parking: SW19 7NL

WIMBLEDON

Home to Elisabeth Beresford's Wombles and the world's most famous tennis tournament, Wimbledon is a large, affluent suburb in southwest London, part of Surrey until 1965 and now within the London borough of Merton. It comprises two very distinct areas: charming Wimbledon village, adjacent to Wimbledon Common, and the town centre surrounding the railway station.

The presence of a hill fort on the common suggests that Wimbledon has been inhabited since at least the Iron Age. It has its first mention in 967, referred to in King Edgar the Peaceful's charter as Wimbedounyng, meaning 'Wynnman's hill'. The manor of Wimbledon was held by the church until 1398, when it was confiscated and became crown property, which it remained until Henry VIII granted it to Thomas Cromwell in 1539 (albeit briefly – Cromwell was beheaded a year later!). In the following centuries ownership switched between various wealthy families, many of whom built large mansions, while the village's rural population coexisted alongside nobility and wealthy City merchants. In 1838, the London and Southwest Railway built a station at the bottom of Wimbledon Hill, which resulted in the town developing rapidly, separate from the original village centre.

Today, Wimbledon is a byword for tennis; the annual Wimbledon Tennis Championships is the oldest tennis tournament in the world and the only Grand Slam still played on grass. But the suburb offers much more than tennis: beautiful Georgian and Victorian architecture; two splendid parks and a vast common; a couple of theatres; and one of the prettiest village centres in London with a wealth of boutiques, cafés, restaurants and bars. One thing Wimbledon has in abundance, which makes this walk especially pleasing, is an overabundance of exceptional pubs, from old-fashioned boozers to stylish gastropubs.

Start Walking…

Emerging from Wimbledon station, you're in the unprepossessing town centre; Wimbledon Village is around half a mile (1km) away up the hill. Turn right on Wimbledon Bridge and immediately on your right is **Kaldi Coffee** ❶ – a good place to perk you up before your walk. Carry on up to the Alexandra pub and cross over to go down Worple Road, past Sainsbury's, to the mini roundabout and turn right into Raymond Road. At the end, where the road turns right, turn left along the alleyway, which cuts through to Sunnyside Passage and Sunnyside. Follow this attractive narrow road to reach The Ridgway, turn right and a short way along on the left is the **Museum of Wimbledon** ❷ (free admission, weekends 2.30-5pm), an absorbing local history museum housed in the original Victorian village hall.

Continue along The Ridgway and turn left onto High Street Wimbledon, which marks the beginning of the village proper, with its cornucopia of designer shops, pubs and restaurants, set among handsome period buildings. The first section, before Church Road, was created 'only' in the mid-19th century; thereafter the buildings are older, reflecting the many grand mansions which once lined Wimbledon's streets. One of the few survivors is **Eagle House** ❸, located on the right just past Lancaster Road. One of the finest Jacobean manor houses in London, Eagle House was built in 1613 for Robert Bell, Master of the Worshipful Company of Girdlers, and co-founder and a director of the British East India Company. Over the years it has been a school, a military academy and an Islamic cultural centre, and it's now divided into luxury apartments.

Wimbledon Village is a foodie's delight with a range of superior eateries (there's even an offshoot of the uber-fashionable Ivy) and superb pubs, including the **Dog & Fox** ❹ on the High Street (adjacent to Wimbledon Village Stables), the **Fire Stables** ❺, a

Wimbledon Village

Southside House

This 17th-century gem of a property was built for Robert Pennington, who commissioned Dutch architects to build it, incorporating an existing farmhouse into its design. The house was later rebuilt in the William and Mary style, but behind the long façade are the old rooms, still with much of the Pennington family's 17th-century furniture, and a superb collection of art and historical objects reflecting centuries of ownership. The house – and enchanting garden – can be visited on a pre-booked guided tour (see http://southsidehouse.com).

gastropub in Church Road with exposed brick, leather armchairs and a contemporary dining room, and, further along the High Street, the popular **Rose & Crown 6**. Opposite the Dog & Fox is the iconic red-brick **Old Fire Station 7**, with a striking clock tower dating from 1890, while next door is **Maison St Cassien 8**, serving Mediterranean and Lebanese cuisine.

Once you reach the Rose & Crown, turn left onto High Street (yes, Wimbledon has two high streets!) and continue to the corner of Wimbledon Common. The High Street (and Southside Common further down) was once lined with mansions, few of which now remain; one survivor is Claremont House (number 44, on the left as you approach the common), built in 1650 by Thomas Hilliard.

Continue along the path that runs parallel with Southside Common – anti-slavery campaigner William Wilberforce once lived at number 6, marked by a plaque – and exit in the corner of the common opposite **King's College School 9**. An independent school housed in a hotchpotch of period and newer buildings, it was founded in 1829 as the junior department of King's College London (it relocated here in 1897). Continue along Woodhayes Road, passing Wright's Alley on the left, an ancient right of way between the common and The Ridgway where you were earlier, where you come to **Southside House 10** (see box).

A short way past Southside House, at number 6 is **Gothic Lodge 11**. Dating from 1763, it's the former home of William Henry Preece (1834-1913), engineer and inventor in the fields of radio and telephony; this was the first house in London to have its own telephone. Retrace your steps to turn left along Crooked Billet, which is lined with former

Cannizaro Park

Cannizaro Park

This lovely Grade II* listed park was a private garden for some 300 years before opening to the public in 1949. Extending to around 35 acres (14ha), it's a 'secret' garden combining great natural beauty with a unique collection of rare and exquisite trees and shrubs, including sassafras, camellia, rhododendron and other ericaceous plants. The park has a large variety of green areas, from expansive lawns and leisurely walks through woodlands, to formal areas such as the sunken garden next to Cannizaro House and the Italian Garden near the pond. (For more information see www.cannizaropark. com.)

Bistro Wimbledon ⑯ , housed in 18th-century Cannizaro House.

Hand in Hand pub

From the park continue along West Side Common into West Place – take a detour on the left to

workmen's cottages and Cinque Cottages – charity almshouses built in 1872 for men in need aged over 55. Follow the road round to the right to pass not one, but two excellent pubs: the **Crooked Billet** ⑫ , a Young's gastropub, and the award-winning **Hand in Hand** ⑬ , dating from 1835 (originally a bakery). At the end of the road turn left on Woodhayes Road and bear left again to West Side Common.

The imposing house immediately on the left behind the lamp-lit gate is **Chester House** ⑭ . Wimbledon's third-oldest building, it dates from around 1700 and was the home of radical politician and reformer John Horne Tooke from 1792 until his death in 1812. A few hundred metres further up on the left is **Cannizaro Park** ⑮ (see box), one of the city's best small parks (free entrance, 8/9am-7pm). The entrance is via the grand gates to the right of the **Hotel du Vin &**

Food & Drink

① **Kaldi Coffee:** A good independent coffee house just outside Wimbledon station (6am-7pm, £).

⑤ **Fire Stables:** Gorgeous gastropub in Church Road with a modern British menu (10am/noon-11pm, £-££).

⑧ **Maison St Cassien:** Friendly café-restaurant in Wimbledon Village popular with tennis stars (7am-6pm, £-££).

⑰ **Fox & Grapes:** Located near Cannizaro Park, this exceptional gastropub is a good place for lunch, particularly on Sundays (8am-11pm, £-££).

Camp Road to visit the admirable **Fox & Grapes** **17**, a superior gastropub – and continue straight ahead at the end to Wimbledon Common. Created in 1871 by an Act of Parliament for public recreation and the preservation of flora and fauna, Wimbledon Common, together with Putney Heath and Putney Lower Common, makes up the largest expanse of heathland in London at 1,136 acres (460ha). It's an important site for the stag beetle, and in the '70s was the home of the Wombles, fictional furry creatures who lived in burrows and recycled rubbish in Elisabeth Beresford's books (and TV series).

Buddhapadipa Temple

One of Europe's few Thai temples, the Buddhapadipa Temple (or Wat Buddhapadipa) was established in 1966 by the London Buddhist Temple Foundation to create a centre for the dissemination of theoretical and practical Buddhist teachings; it's now one of Europe's most important Buddhist training centres. The grounds – open daily 9.30am-5/6pm – cover approximately 4 acres (1.6ha), where the beautiful Uposatha Hall (temple) is situated on an ornamental lake, with a small grove, flower garden and an orchard. (For more information see www. watbuddhapadipa.org.)

Follow the path north across the common – a nice walk though there's not much to see apart from some silver birch trees – to Windmill Road and the white sails of **Wimbledon Windmill Museum** **18** (late Mar to late Oct, Sat 2-5pm, Sun 11am-5pm, free entry). The museum is housed in a windmill built in 1817 by Charles March to grind flour for local residents. It operated until 1864 and has been a museum since 1976, with the sails restored to working order in 1999. There's also a tearoom (9am-5.15/6.15pm) and toilets. From the windmill head east along Windmill Road and turn right on Parkside, passing Parkside Hospital, and go left down Calonne Road to see the **Buddhapadipa Temple** **19** (see box, left).

Continue to the end of Calonne Road and go right on Burghley Road. After 150m, you cross Marryat Road which leads (on the left) to the **All England Lawn Tennis and Croquet Club** **20**, home of the annual Wimbledon Championships in June-July. The next junction is with Church Road, and another detour, some 150m up on the right, brings you to the **Old Rectory** **21**. Built in the early 1500s, it's Wimbledon's oldest inhabited building. Henry VIII gave it to his sixth wife Catherine Parr in 1543, and it was the country retreat of Sir William Cecil, 1st Lord Burghley, in the 1550s; more recently it was owned by Brian May from rock band Queen. The house was a near ruin in the 19th century, but after decades of restoration was sold for £17.5 million in 2013.

Cross Church Road to St Mary's Road and go left at the second of two mini roundabouts to visit **St Mary's Church** 22 (see box, below). Three of the four large manor houses that once graced Wimbledon stood in this area – one belonged to the Duchess of Marlborough, another to the Spencer family – while the fourth house, built by Sir Theodore Janssen in around 1720, was just to the south near Alan Road. All but the Old Rectory have been demolished.

at the Alexandra pub) has tasty burgers and a nice roof terrace – to visit **St Mark's Church** 24 , a contemporary tent-like building which replaced a Victorian church that burnt down in 1966. The church has some striking stained glass windows and an attractive garden. Follow the path around the church to Alexandra Road, and go right to return to Wimbledon Hill Road. Wimbledon station – and the end of the walk – is a short way along on the left.

St Mary's Church

Designed by Sir George Gilbert Scott (1811-1878), St Mary's is a striking Anglican parish church, built of knapped flint and limestone; it's the fourth recorded church on the site since 1086. Scott had a strict budget for the work and incorporated parts of an earlier Georgian building, adding a new tower and spire (196ft/60m), while the existing windows were enlarged and given their present perpendicular form. Along with Chiswick and Hampstead graveyards, St Mary's churchyard has the highest concentration of listed monuments in Greater London, including a number of ostentatious memorials. Of particular note is the mausoleum of Sir Joseph William Bazalgette (1819-1891), the engineer responsible for building London's sewer system and Embankment.

St Mary's Church

Wend your way to the end of St Mary's Road and turn right on Woodside then left onto Wimbledon Hill Road, as you return to the modern part of town. Turn left down St Mark's Place – where **The Loft** 23 (upstairs

The Best of London: Capital of Cool

ISBN: 978-1-909282-92-6, 256 pages, £11.99, David Hampshire

There are great world cities, from classical capitals to modern metropolises, and then there's London – the yardstick by which other cities are measured. It has the most astonishing ability to reinvent itself, always staying one step ahead of the pack, a magnet for creatives – be they writers or artists, designers or thinkers – and a melting pot of cultures from around the globe. New York may be hip, Paris may be chic, but London is surely the Capital of Cool.

London for Foodies, Gourmets & Gluttons

ISBN: 978-1-909282-76-6, 288 pages £11.95, David Hampshire & Graeme Chesters

London for Foodies, Gourmets & Gluttons is much more than simply a directory of cafés, markets, restaurants and food shops. It features many of the city's best artisan producers and purveyors, plus a wealth of classes where you can learn how to prepare and cook food like the experts, appreciate fine wines and brew coffee like a barista. And when you're too tired to cook or just want to treat yourself, we'll show you great places where you can enjoy everything from tea and cake to a tasty street snack; a pie and a pint to a glass of wine and tapas; and a quick working lunch to a full-blown gastronomic extravaganza.

London's Best Shops & Markets

ISBN: 978-1-909282-81-0, 256 pages £12.95, David Hampshire

The UK is a nation of diehard shoppers. Retail therapy is the country's favourite leisure activity – an all-consuming passion – and London is its beating heart. It's one of the world's most exciting shopping cities, packed with grand department stores, trend-setting boutiques, timeless traditional traders, edgy concept stores, absorbing antiques centres, eccentric novelty shops, exclusive purveyors of luxury goods, mouth-watering food emporiums, bustling markets and much more.

see www.survivalbooks.net

INDEX

London's Secrets

LONDON'S HIDDEN SECRETS

ISBN: 978-1-907339-40-0

£10.95, 320 pages, colour

Graeme Chesters

A unique and unusual guide to London's hidden and lesser-known sights not found in standard guidebooks. London is a city with a cornucopia of secret places, being ancient, vast and in a constant state of flux.

London's Hidden Secrets takes you off the beaten path to seek out the more unusual places that often fail to register on the radar of both visitors and residents alike, and aims to sidestep the chaos and queues of London's tourist-clogged attractions and visit its quirkier, more mysterious side.

LONDON'S SECRETS: BIZARRE & CURIOUS

ISBN: 978-1-909282-58-2

£11.95, 320 pages, colour

Graeme Chesters

London is a city with 2,000 years of history, over which it has accumulated a wealth of odd and strange buildings, monuments, statues, street trivia and museum exhibits, to name just a few examples.

This book seeks out the city's most bizarre and curious sights and tells the often fascinating story behind them, from the Highgate vampire to the arrest of a dead man, a legal brothel and a former Texas embassy to Roman bikini bottoms and poetic manhole covers, from London's hanging gardens to a restaurant where you dine in the dark.

LONDON'S SECRET PLACE

ISBN: 978-1-907339-92-9

£10.95, 320 pages, colour

Graeme Chesters & David Hampshire

London is one of the world's leading tourist destinations with wealth of world-class attractions amazing museums and galleries beautiful parks and gardens, stunning palaces and grand houses, and much, much more. These are covered in a plethora of excellent tourist guides and online, and need no introduction here.

Not so well known are Londor numerous smaller attractions, most of which are neglected by the throngs who descend upon the tourist-clogged major sights. What London's Secret Places does is seek out the city lesser-known, but no less worth 'hidden' attractions.

see www.londons-secrets.com